AF594117

A SENSE SUBLIME

A SENSE SUBLIME

RICHARD QUINNEY

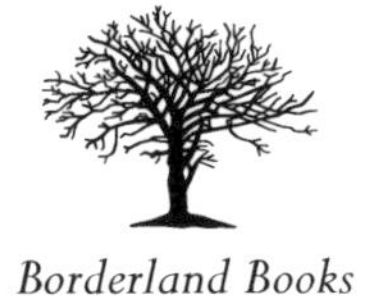

Borderland Books

Published by Borderland Books, Madison, WI
www.borderlandbooks.net

Publisher's Cataloging-In-Publication Data
Quinney, Richard.
A sense sublime / Richard Quinney.— 1st ed.
Includes bibliographical references
ISBN: 978-0-9835174-4-3

1. Illinois—Pictorial works. 2. Outdoor photography—Illinois. 3. Country life—Illinois—DeKalb—20th century—Pictorial works. 4. Sublime, The—Pictorial works. 5. Sublime, The—Quotations. 6. Quinney, Richard—Photograph collections. I. Title.

TR659.5 .Q562 2013
779/.3/773 2013900109

Printed in the United States of America
First edition
Designed by Ken Crocker
Printed by Worzalla Printing
Typeset in Sabon

To the attentive eye, each moment of the year has its own beauty, and in the same field, it beholds, every hour, a picture which was never seen before, and which shall never be seen again. The heavens change every moment, and reflect their glory or gloom on the plains beneath.

Ralph Waldo Emerson

Contents

Preface

This book is a record of a life lived during the last years of the twentieth century. Eighteen years of my life, between 1983 and 2001, were spent on the northern edge of the tallgrass prairie of Illinois, where prairie land gives way to the glaciated hills of Wisconsin. Eventually I would cross the border to be near the family farm. These years at century's end could easily be imagined as the years of waiting for the call that would finally define my life. But let us think of these years as a dynamic and vital time, even in the waiting. I was the explorer, with open mind and open heart, continuing a journey of uncertain destination. These were the years of my life as a camera.

I walked the streets and byways of DeKalb, where I lived, and I traveled the country roads of the county. The landscape seemed of transcendent quality, having to do with the line of the horizon, the meeting of land and sky, shadows in the snow along a fence line, the dark passages into abandoned buildings, the drift of clouds over fields, the cemeteries that haunt the landscape, the weathered houses and barns of earlier settlers, the freight trains speeding through town day and night, and the cover of snow all winter long. I watched the rising and passing of all things, giving attention to the wonder of daily existence. A photograph now and then, a few notes made to the day, a life being lived as the years passed.

The photographs, from the last decade of the century, document the passing of the seasons and the years. Accompanying the photographs are notes from the journals that I was keeping as I was photographing. My life, in words and images, during the eighteen years can be found in a series of memoirs, published as *Journey to a Far Place, For the Time Being, Borderland, Once Again the Wonder, Where Yet the Sweet Birds Sing,* and *Tales from the Middle Border.* These are my ethnographies, my field notes, and my stories of daily life lived both in solitude and in the company and care of family and friends.

The absence of fellow human beings in my photographs does not signal a lack of human interest and concern. To the contrary, the landscapes I saw and preserved on film are filled with recognition of the human condition. Photographs cannot be appreciated without an awareness of the landscapes that we humans have created. These black-and-white photographs explore the light and darkness and the shadows that we experience and know in our human existence.

Photographing—the act of framing portions of the world in the viewfinder—was of primary importance during my eighteen years in DeKalb. I lived to photograph, and I photographed to live—stated dramatically. This is photography of consequence. The resulting photographs accompanied by field notes and the words of others, as epigraphs for the photographs, are the artifacts of this life lived in a particular time and place. They are the artifacts of the one who used a camera as a way of being in the world. They are the instruments of survival.

Artifacts of any kind can never convey fully the personal and social substance of a time and place. Historians and archaeologists must make inferences from the materials unearthed. I had moved back to the Midwest to accept a professorship at Northern Illinois University and to be near the farm. Not evident are some facts: I visited my mother often on the farm with my family, my younger daughter completed school and left home for college, I was teaching sociology courses each semester and writing scholarly articles and books, I traveled to Europe and Asia several times, my marriage ended and I eventually remarried, I became a grandfather, I was diagnosed with chronic lymphocytic leukemia and began treatments that continue to this day, I retired from teaching at the university, my mother died, and my wife and I moved north to Wisconsin. The photographs provide the viewer with evidence of the importance of the camera in the living of daily life.

My spiritual life, as the century was drawing to an end, was that of experiencing the sublime in everyday life. I was working in the long tradition of transcendental writers, romantic poets, and landscape painters, and all who would be close to the mystery of human existence. The act of perceiving—and creating—expands the spirit of the artist. The sacred and the profane are joined as one. The spiritual eye of the photographer beheld the landscape with a sense of the sublime.

We begin with the wonder of existence. A meditation on the mysteries of life. The photographs and writings are the remains of a life once lived, lived in the company of family and a community. In the end, imagine that the photographer was happy in his work, traveling daily the highways and byways of a place that for a while was known as home.

Photographs and Epigraphs

1. Elm and Mulberry

The light died in the low clouds. Falling snow drank in the dusk. Shrouded in silence the branches wrapped me in their peace. When the boundaries were erased, once again the wonder: that I exist.

Dag Hammarskjöld

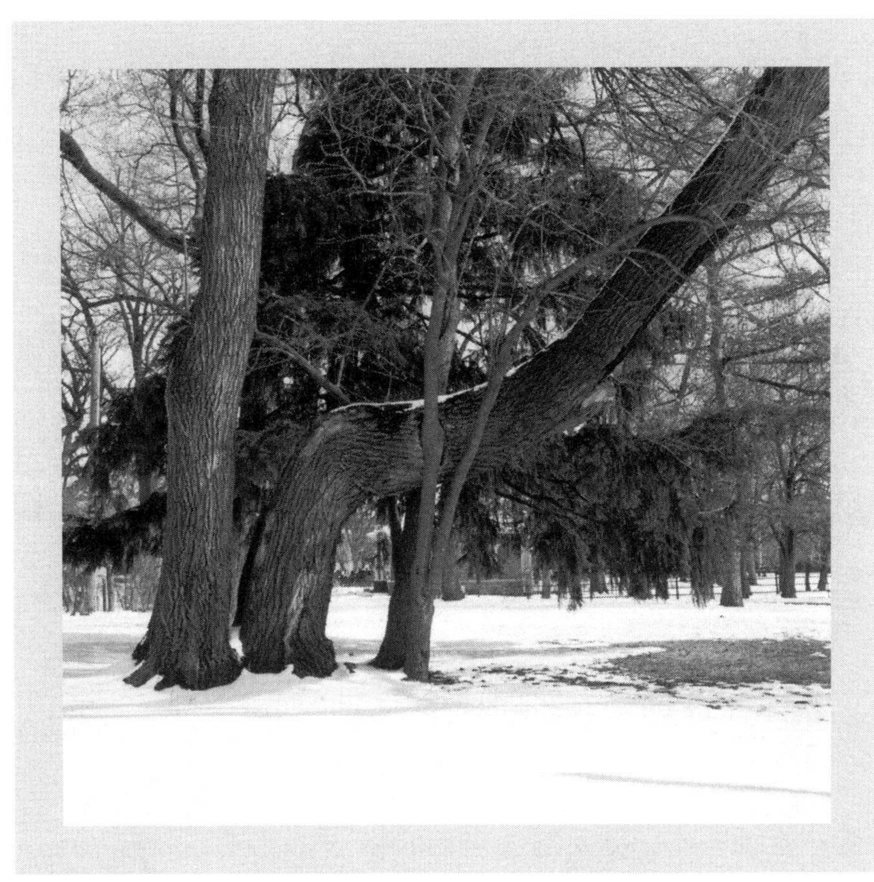

2. Writing Desk

When they bring you to trial and hand you over, do not worry beforehand about what you are to say; but say whatever is given you at that time, for it is not you who speak, but the Holy Spirit.

Mark 13:11

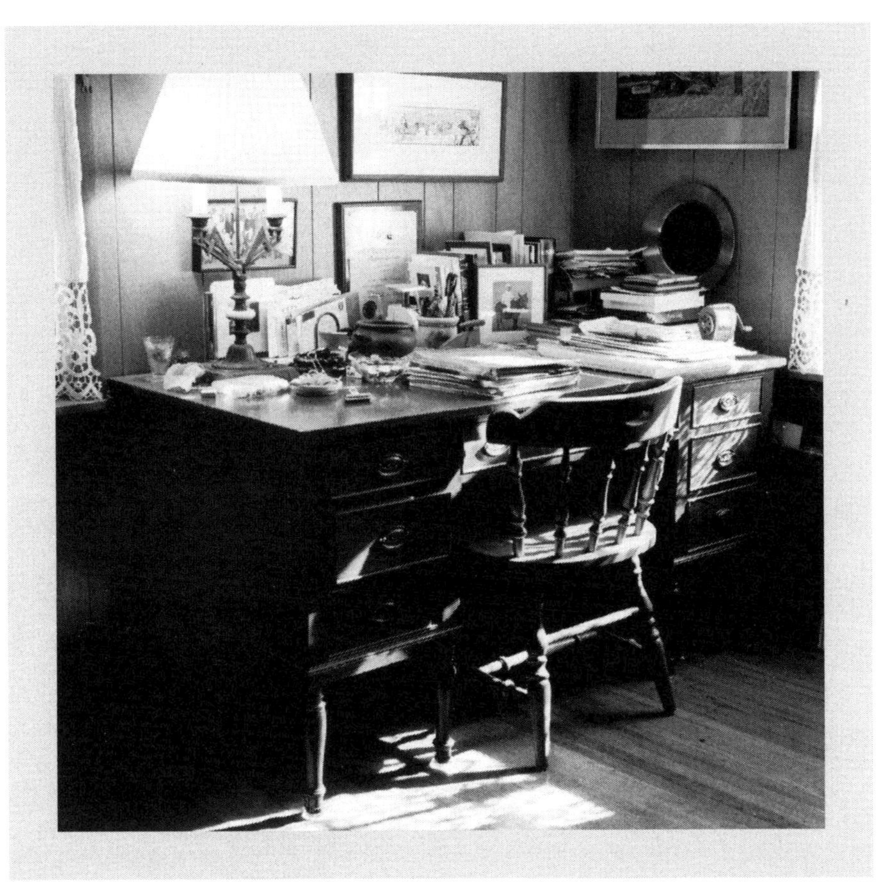

3. Living Room

Those who realize that all life is one
Are at home everywhere and see themselves
In all beings.

Taittiriya Upanishad

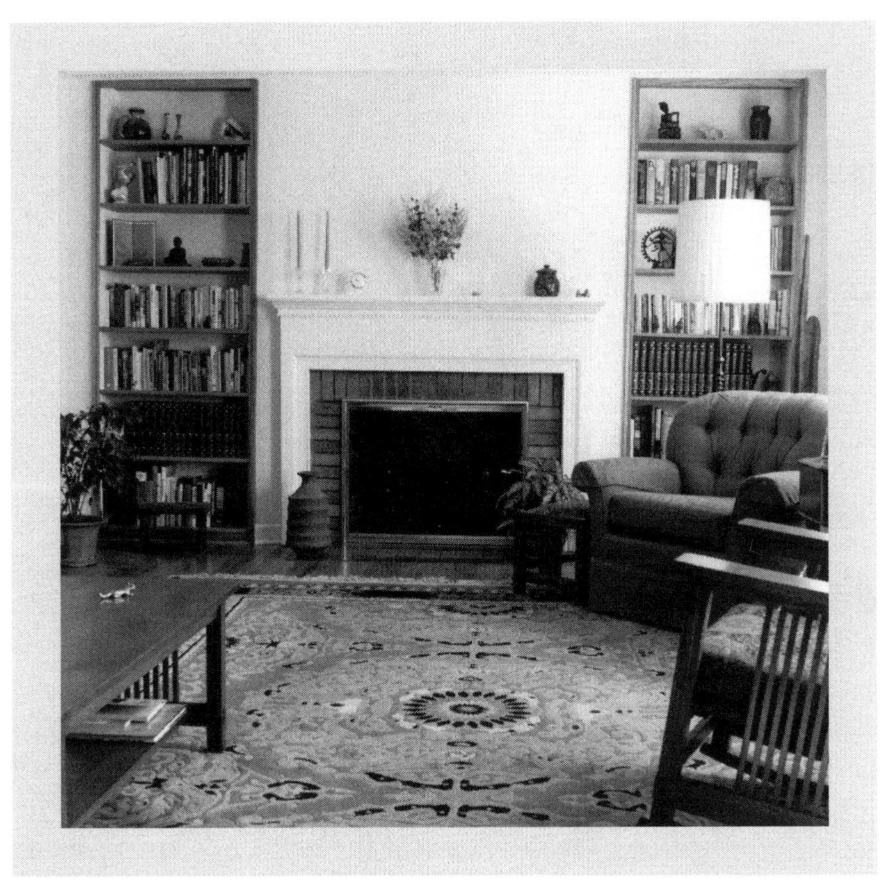

4. Willow at the Lagoon

I once was lost, but now am found,
Was blind, but now I see.

John Newton

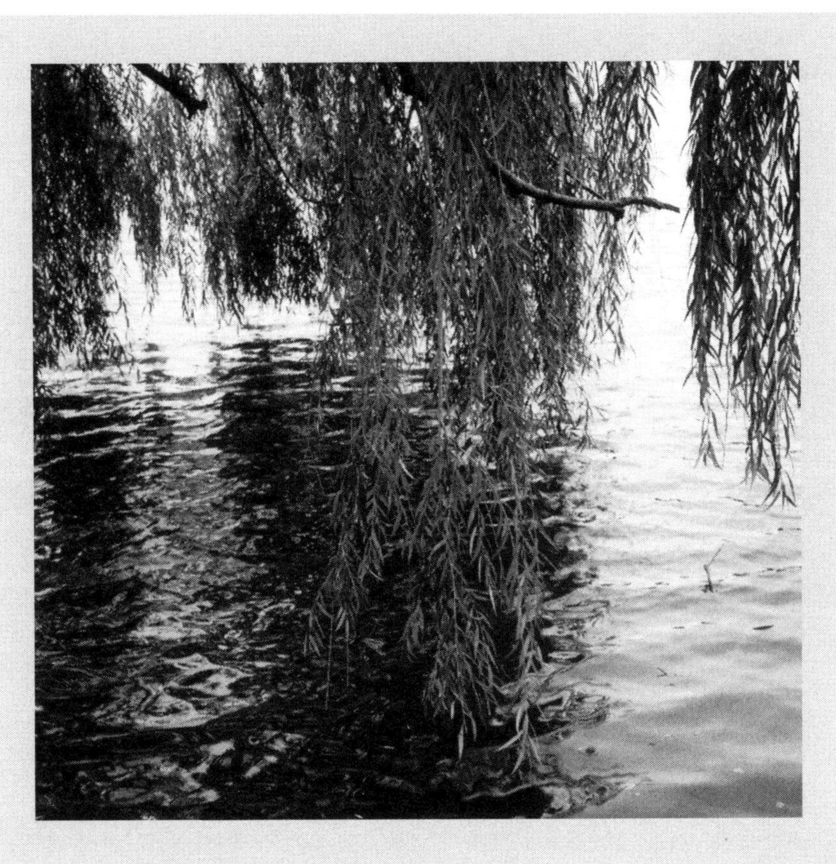

5. Windmill

Those who worship me and meditate on me constantly, without any other thought, I will provide for all their needs.

Bhagavad Gita

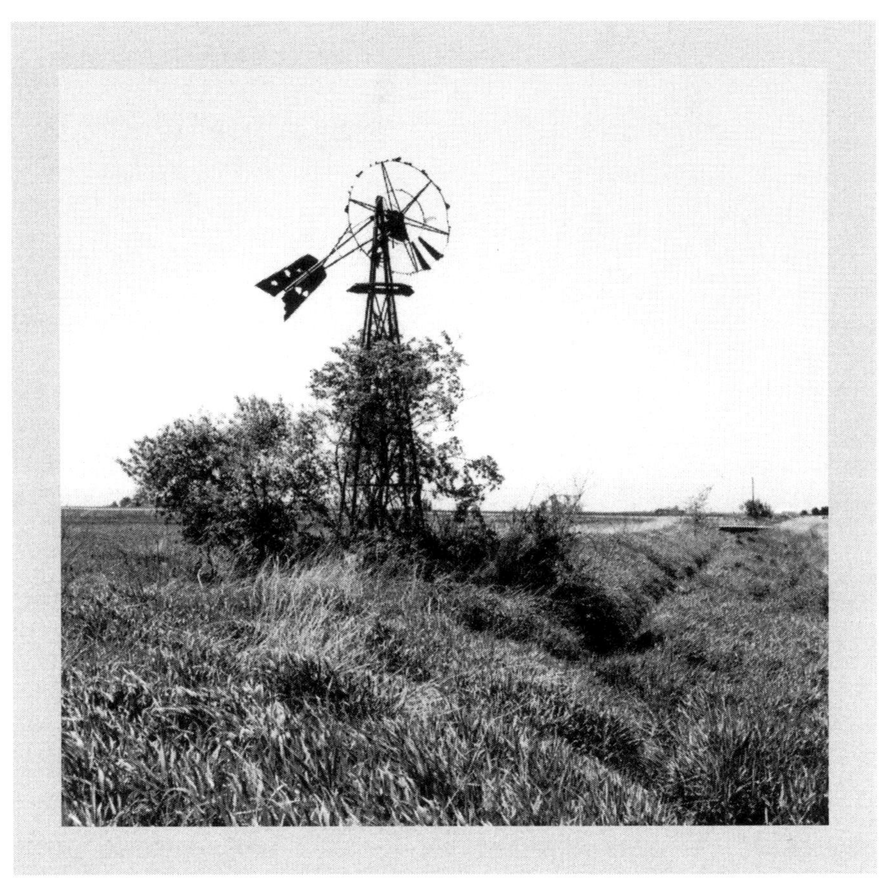

6. A Cow in Water

The eye with which I see God is the same as the eye with which God sees me.

Meister Eckhart

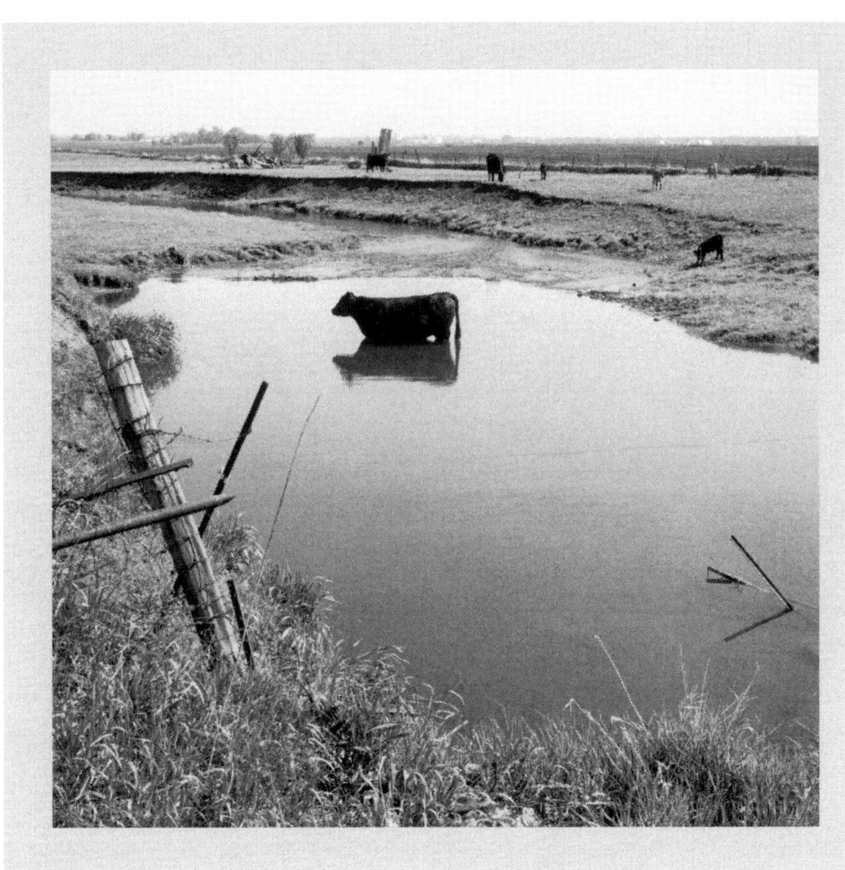

7. Three Trees

Know that everything is the Self.
Rid yourself of all purpose.
And be happy.

Ashtavakra Gita

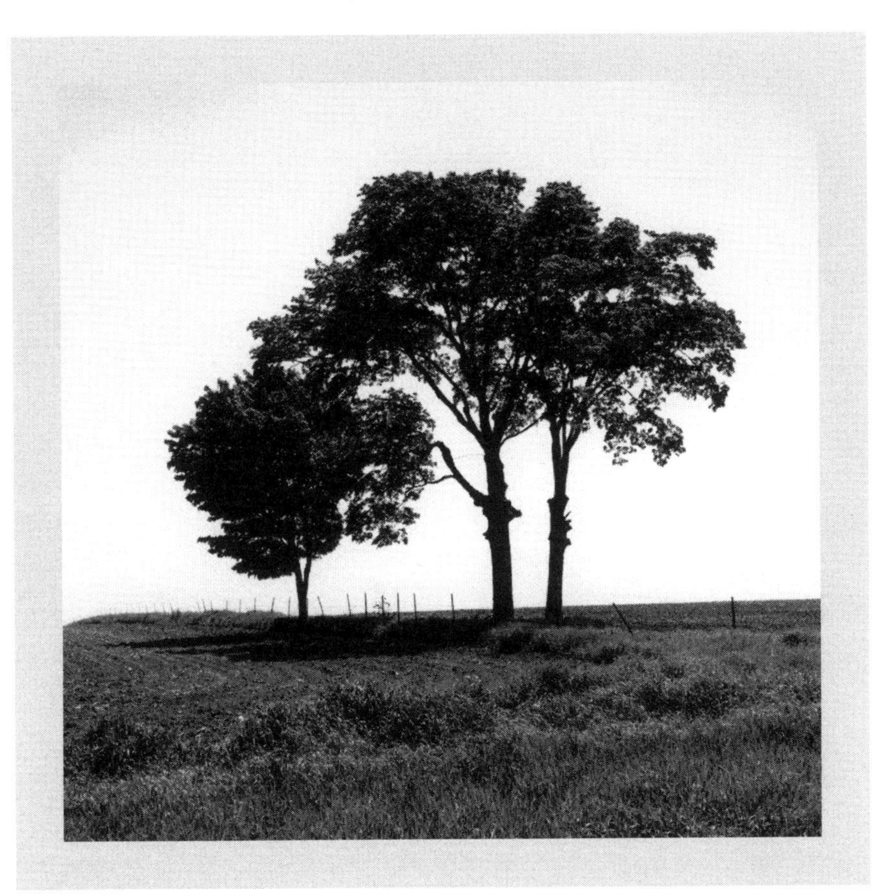

8. Crop Duster

Whatever is fitted in any sort to excite the ideas of pain and danger, that is to say, whatever is in any sort terrible, or is conversant with terrible objects, or operates in a manner analogous to terror, is a source of the sublime.

Edmund Burke

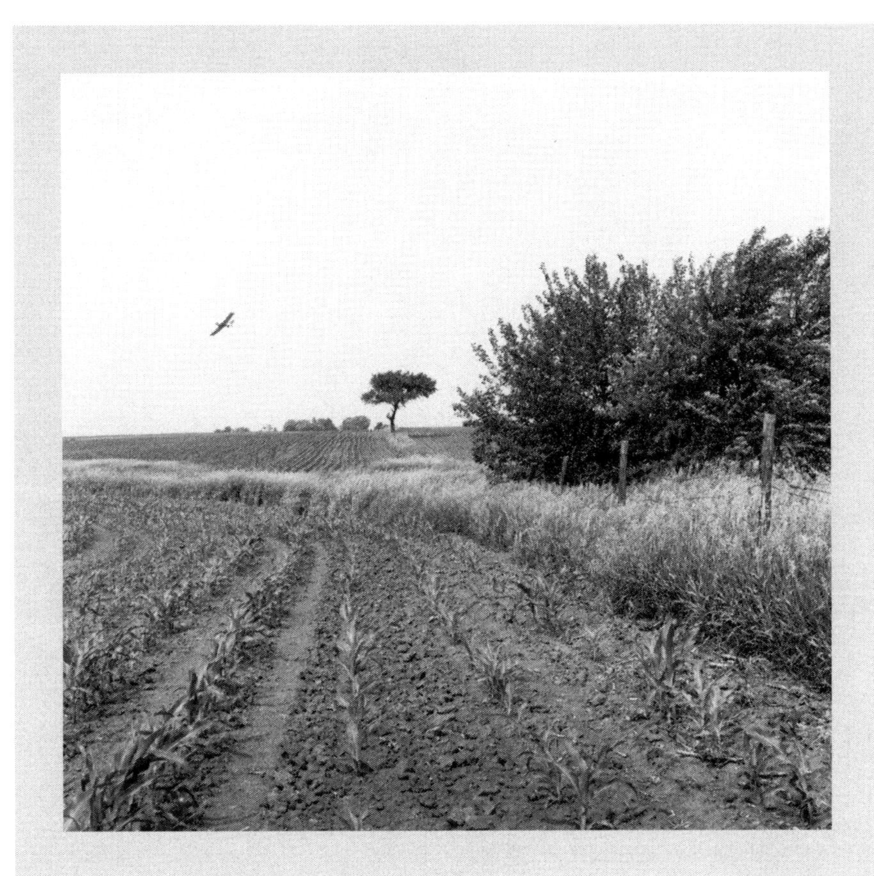

9. Saint Mary's Cemetery

All seems eternal now.

Percy Shelley

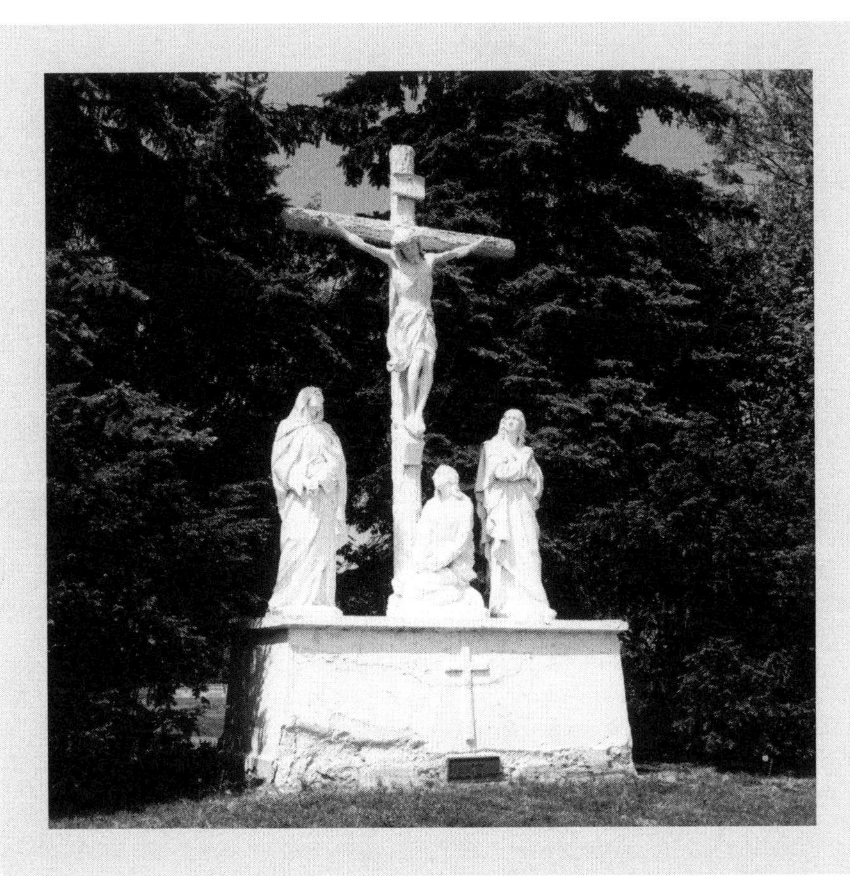

10. Grain Elevator on Highway 64

And I have felt
A presence that disturbs me with the joy
Of elevated thoughts; a sense sublime.

William Wordsworth

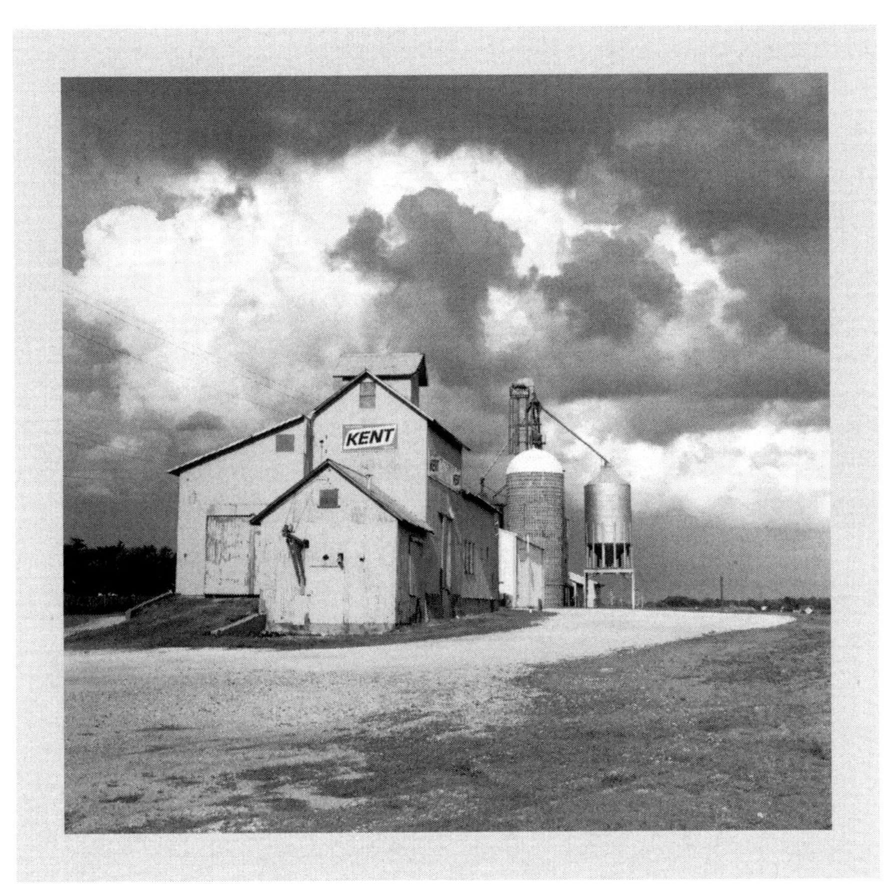
KENT

11. Abandoned Farm on Old State Road

Days and months are travelers of eternity. So are the years that pass by. Those who steer a boat across the sea, or drive a horse over the earth till they succumb to the weight of years, spend every minute of their lives traveling.

Matsuo Bashō

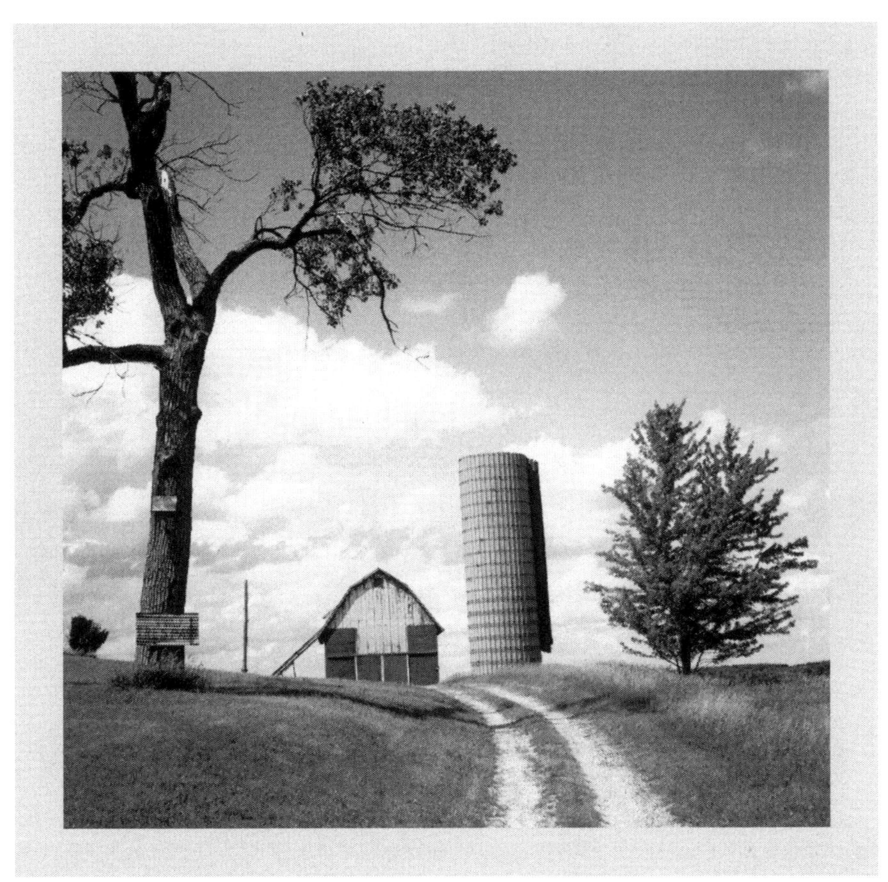

12. Malta Grain Elevator

To love the world you have to first learn how to love your own self. If you love yourself then you love the whole world, because your self includes everything.

Lal Poonja

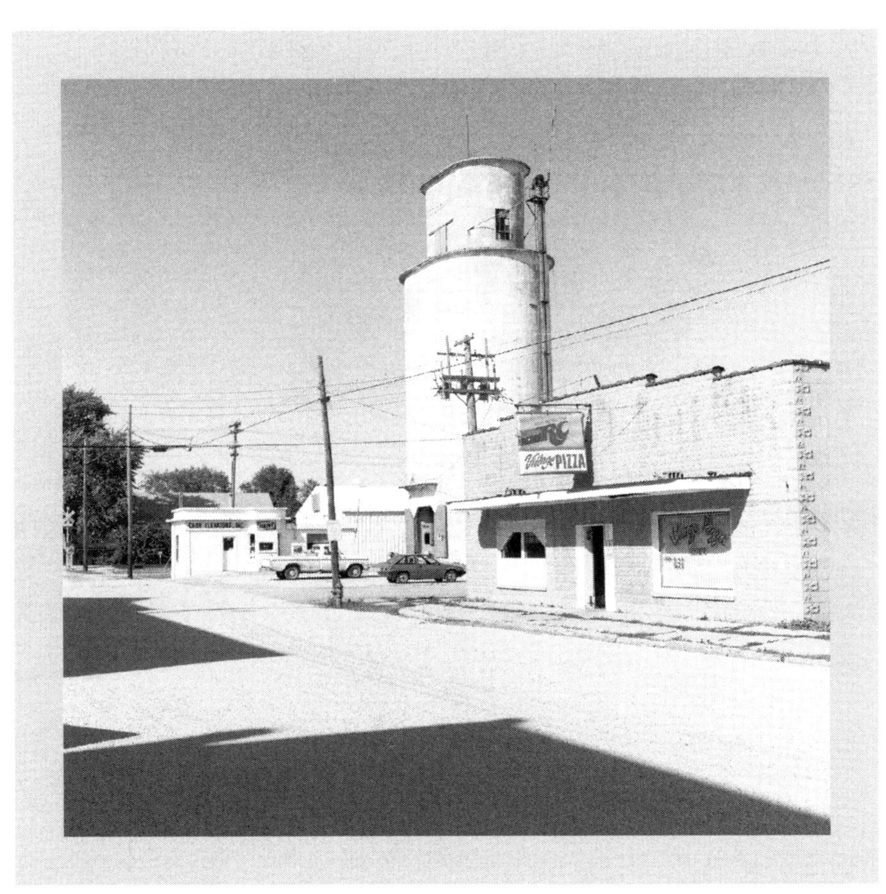
RC
Village PIZZA

13. Farm in Ruins on Cherry Valley Road

That what we feel of sorrow and despair
From ruin and from change, and all the grief
The passing shows of being leave behind,
Appeared an idle dream that could not live
Where meditation was. I turned away,
And walked along my road in happiness.

William Wordsworth

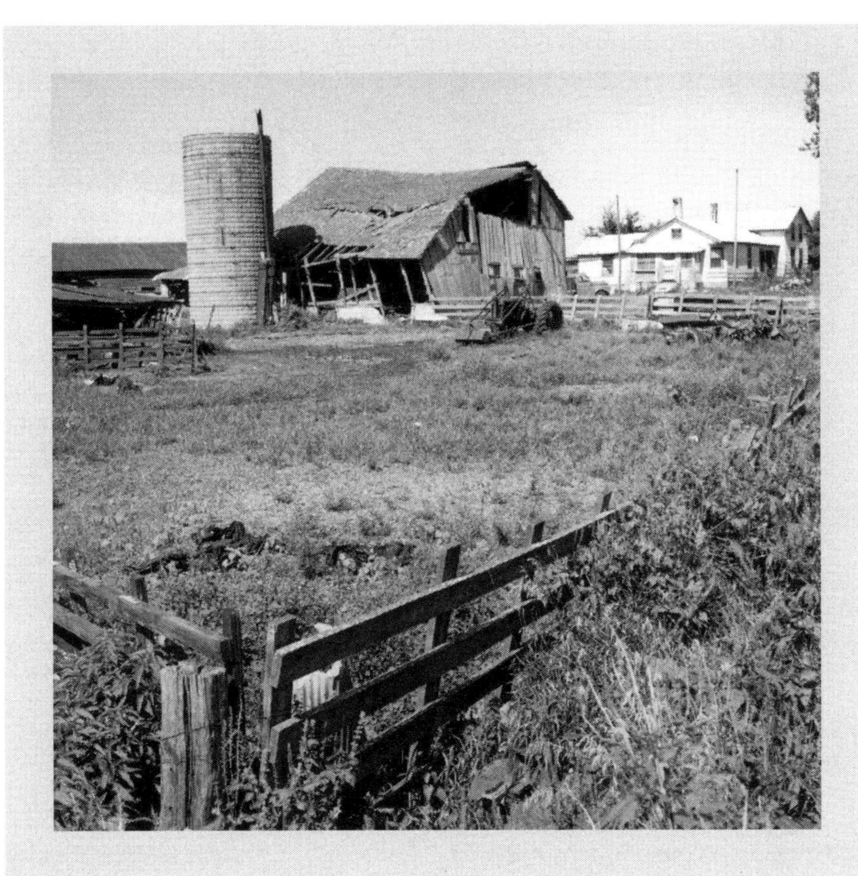

14. Cemetery on Annie Glidden Road

If you attain real, true perception and understanding, birth and death can't affect you—you are free to go or stay.

Zen Master Linji

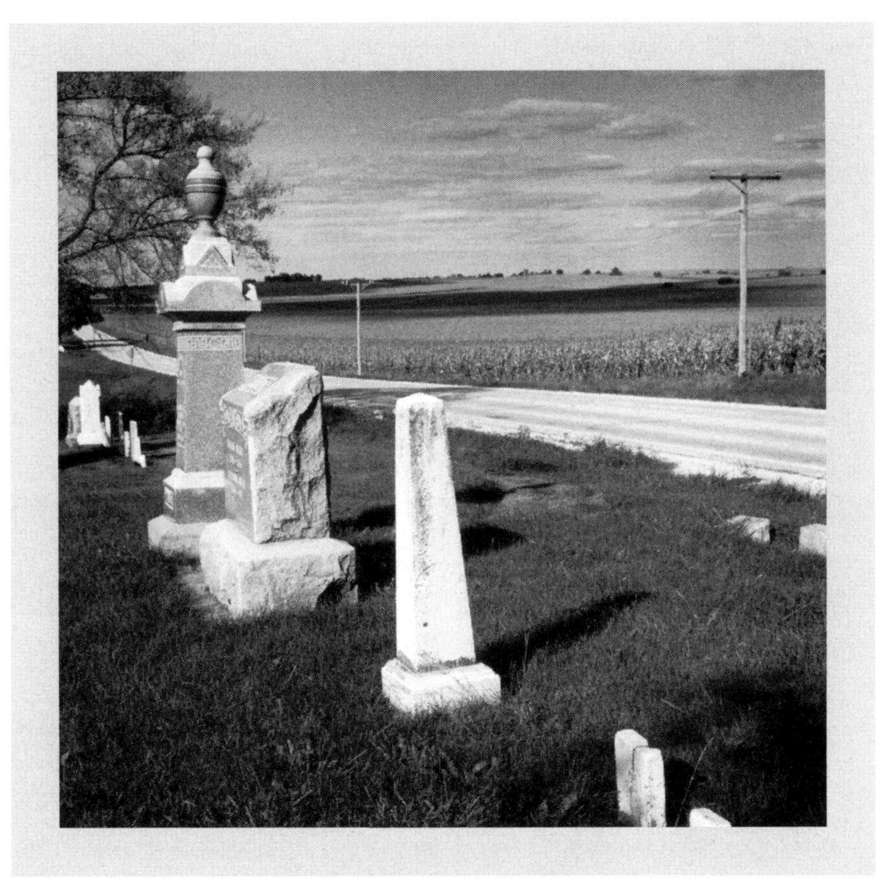

15. Farm in Ruins at the Edge of Town

The effect it produces upon me is not to restore what has been abolished (by time, by distance) but to attest that what I see has indeed existed.

Roland Barthes

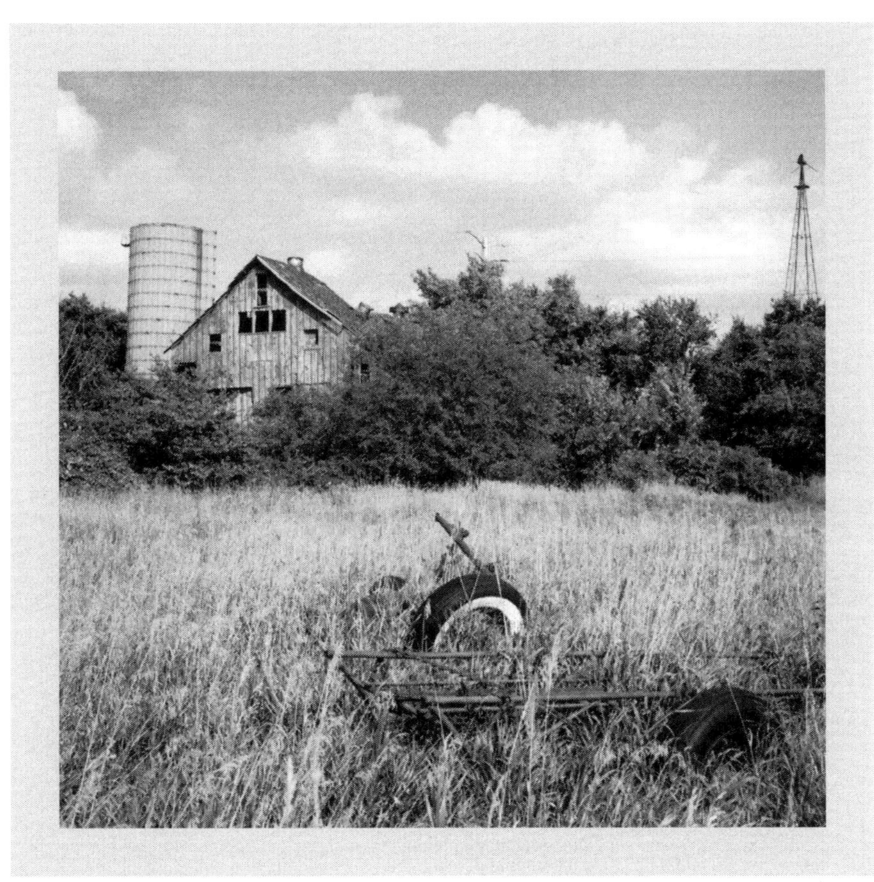

16. Vacant Farmstead on Derby Line Road

True mastery can be gained
by letting things go their own way.
It can't be gained by interfering.

Lao-tzu

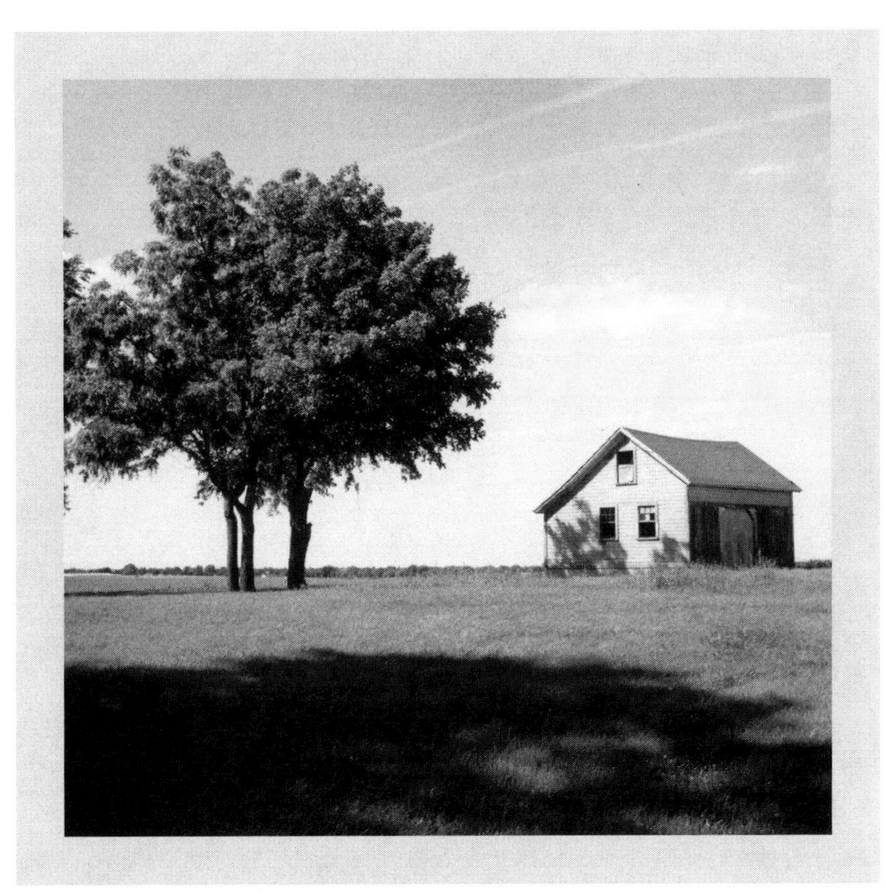

17. Self-Portrait from Lucinda Bridge

Please call me by my true names,
so I can hear all my cries and my laughs at once,
so I can see that my joy and pain are one.

Thich Nhat Hanh

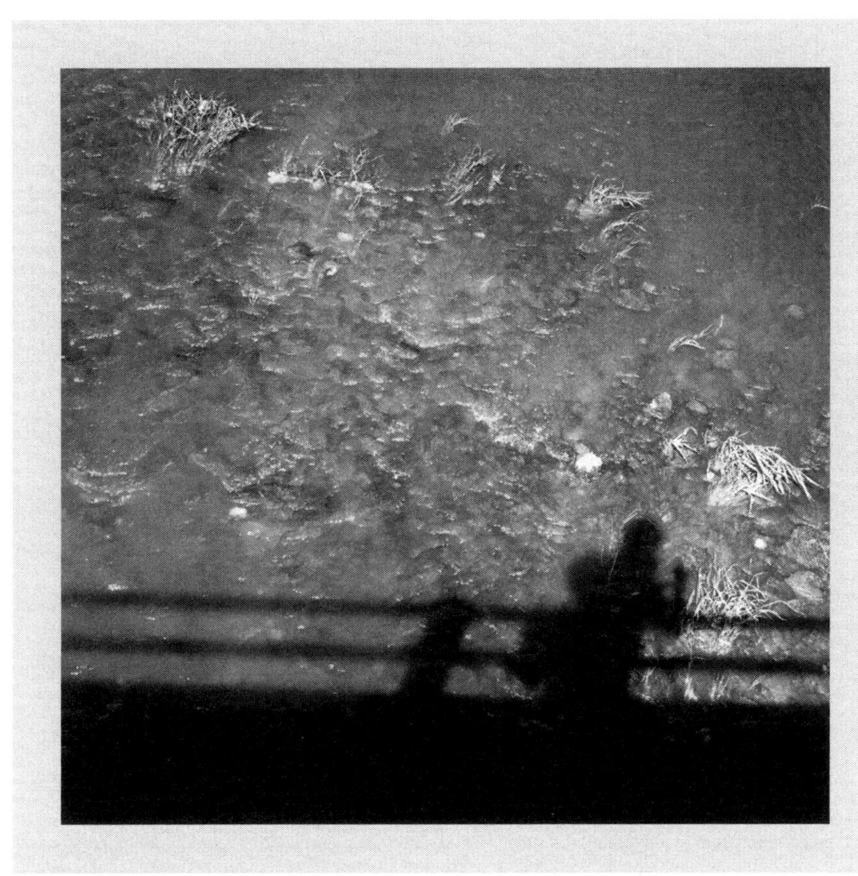

18. Limestone Quarry on Quarry Road

Realize that which pervades the universe and is indestructible; no power can affect this unchanging, imperishable reality.

Bhagavad Gita

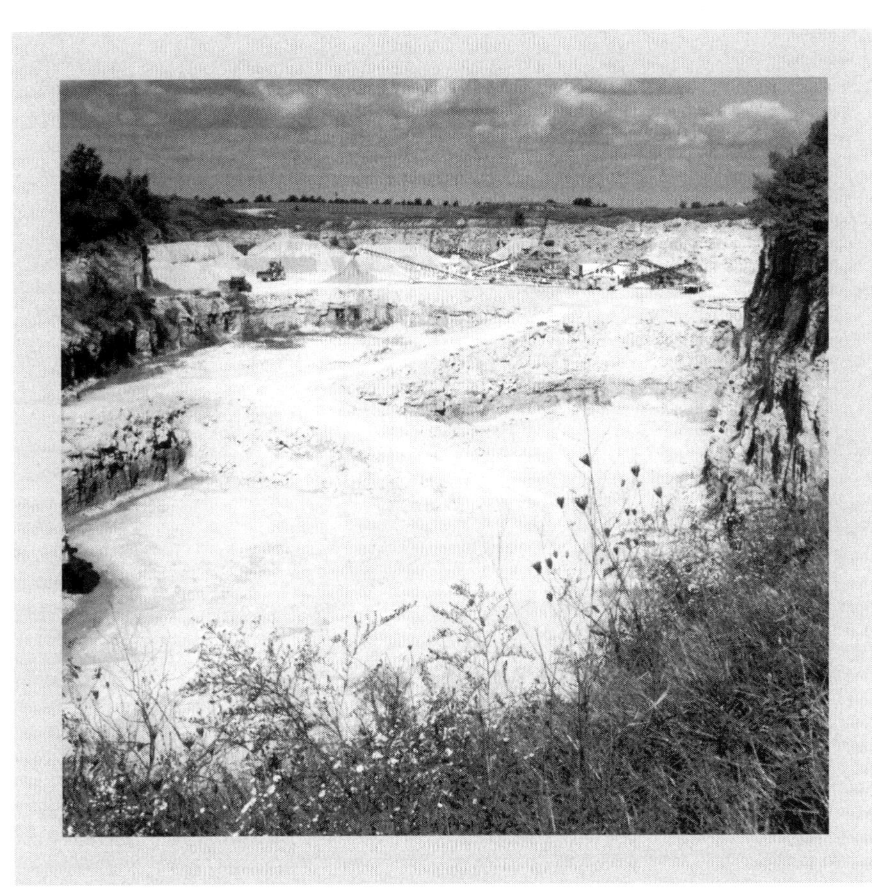

19. Upstairs Window

There is no greater joke than this: that being the Reality ourselves, we seek to gain Reality. A day will dawn when you will yourself laugh at your effort. That which is on the day of laughter is also now.

Ramana Maharshi

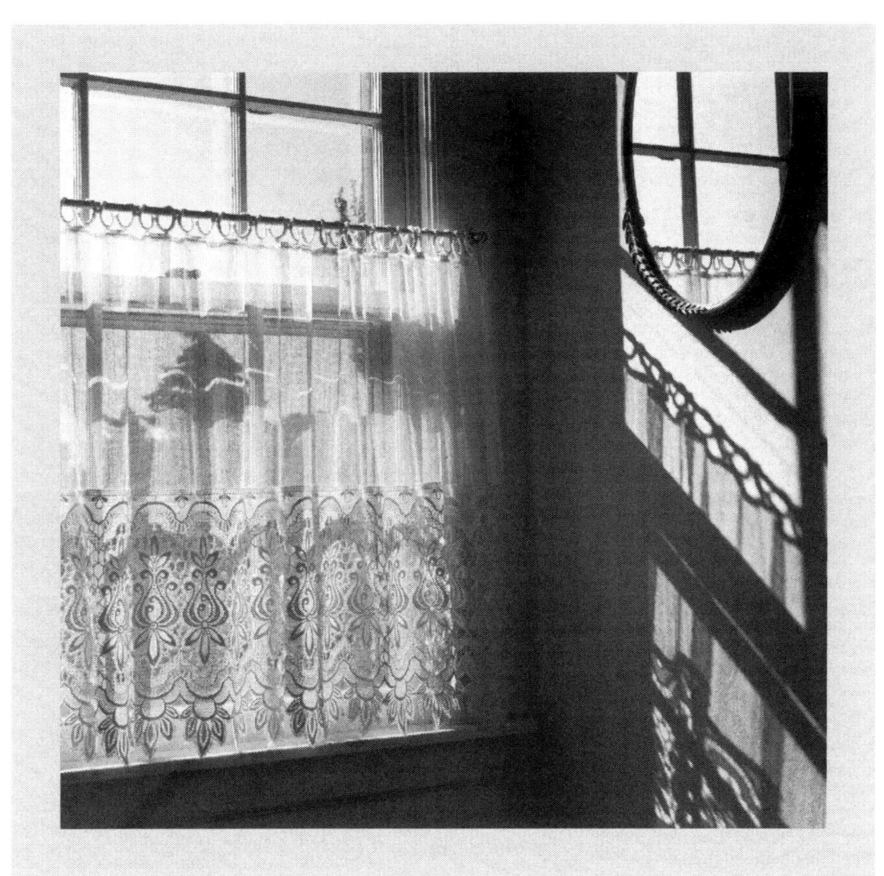

20. Shabbona Lake

What would the world be, once bereft
Of wet and of wildness? Let them be left,
O let them be left, wildness and wet;
Long live the weeds and the wilderness yet.

Gerard Manley Hopkins

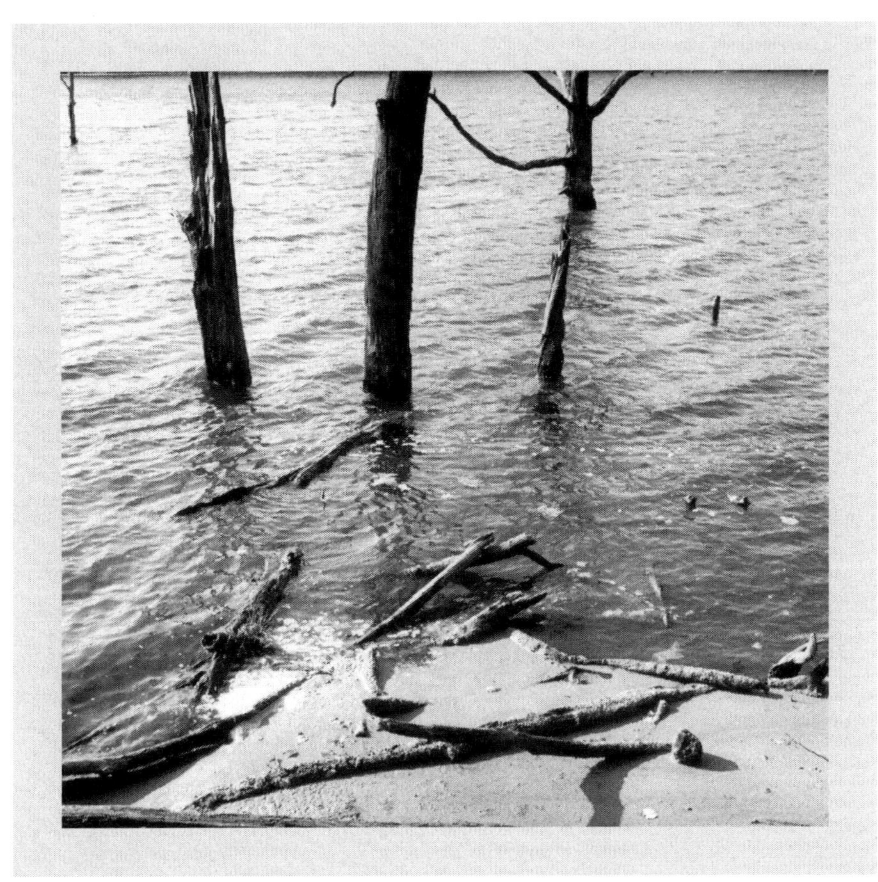

21. Shabbona Grain Elevator

The true harvest of my daily life is somewhat as intangible and indescribable as the tints of morning or evening. It is a little stardust caught, a segment of the rainbow which I have clutched.

Henry David Thoreau

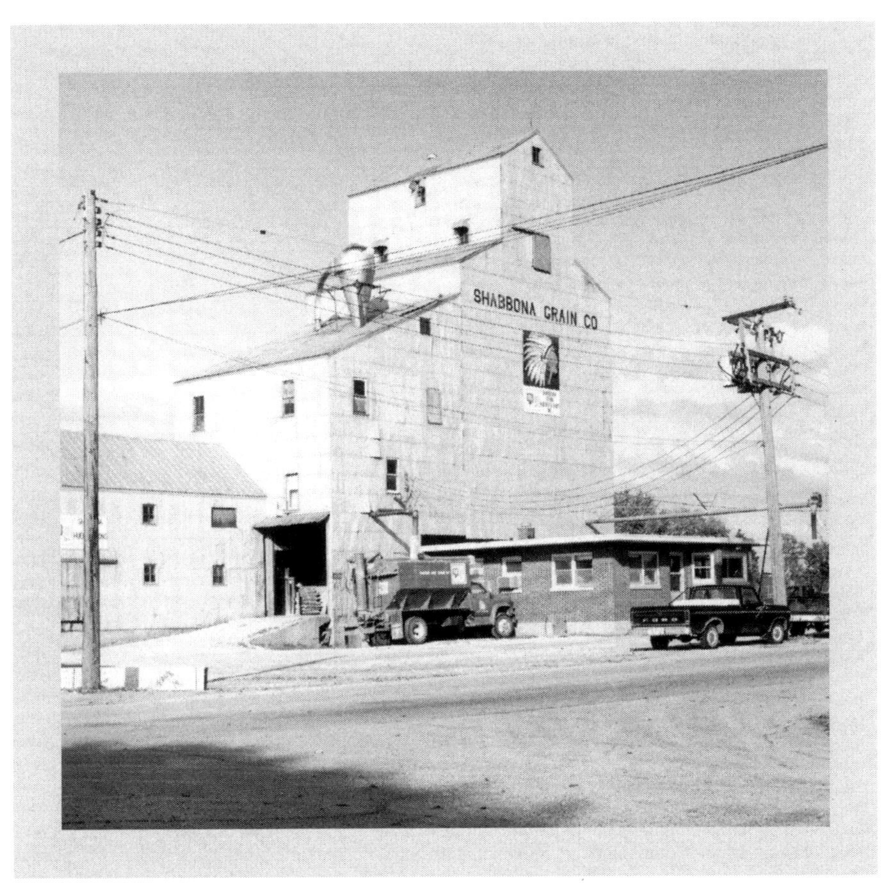
SHABBONA GRAIN CO

22. Cornfield East of Shabbona

The romantic attention is fixed wherever earth and sky meet because that is the break, the seam if you will, where sublimity can be achieved.

James B. Twitchell

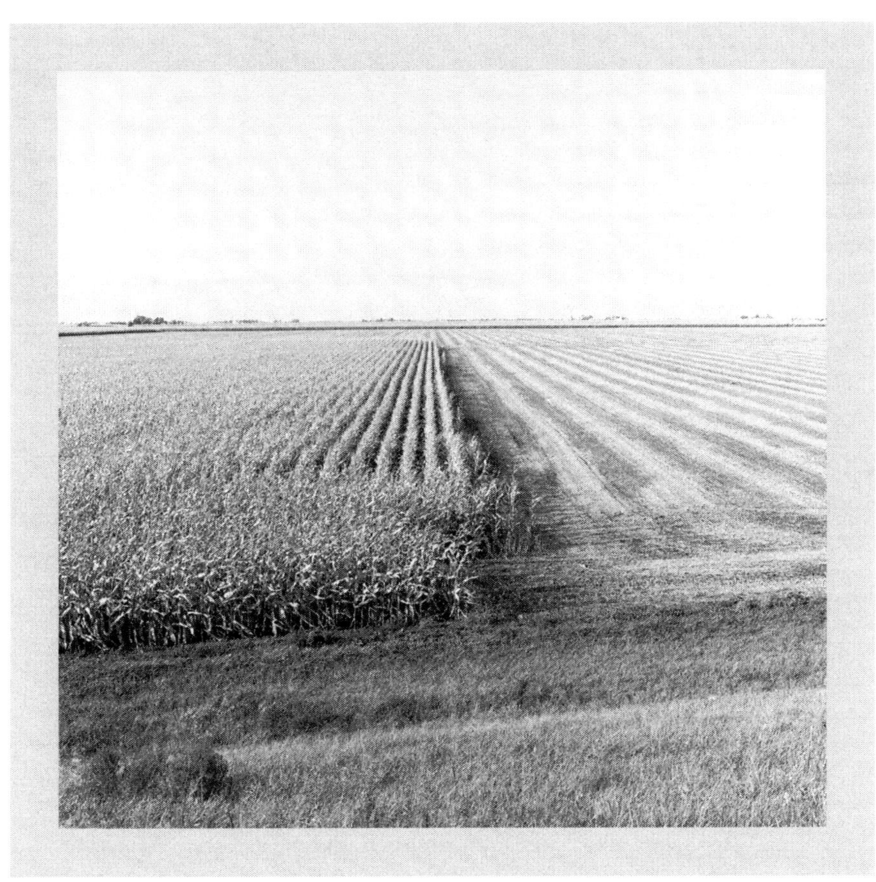

23. Merritt Prairie on Keslinger Road

Stieglitz asked him, "Have you been in love?" And when White answered that, yes he had, Stieglitz said, "Then you can photograph."

James Baker Hall

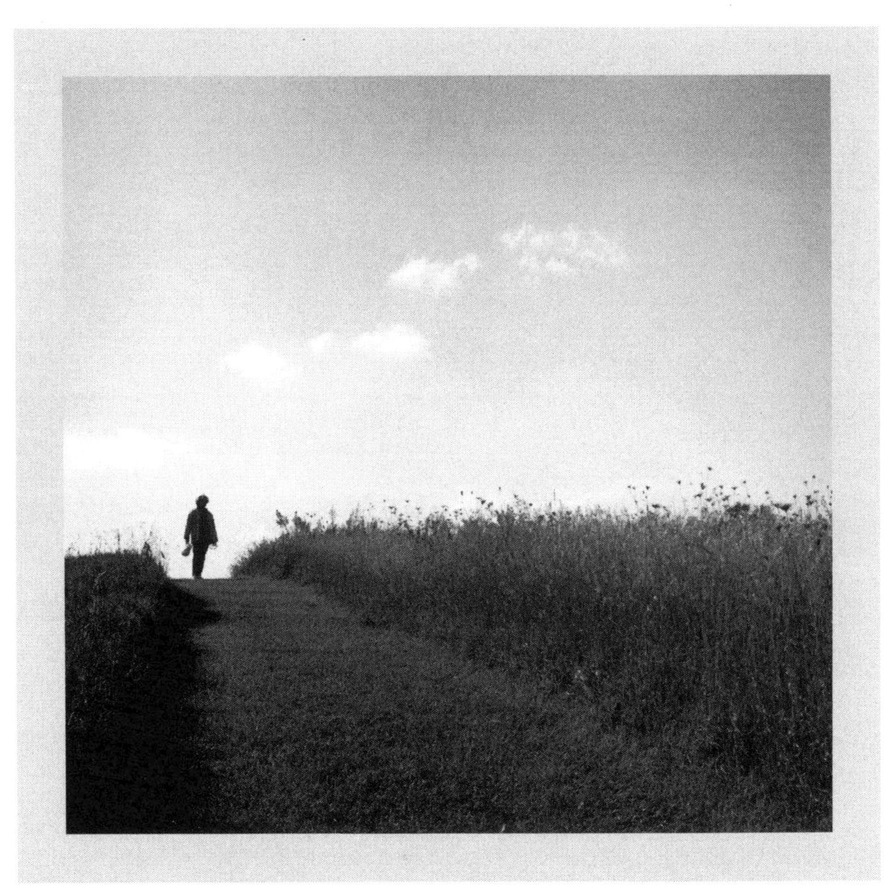

24. Mailboxes at Waterman Road

On the road again.
Goin' places I've never been.
Seein' things that I may never see again,
And I can't wait to get on the road again.

Willie Nelson

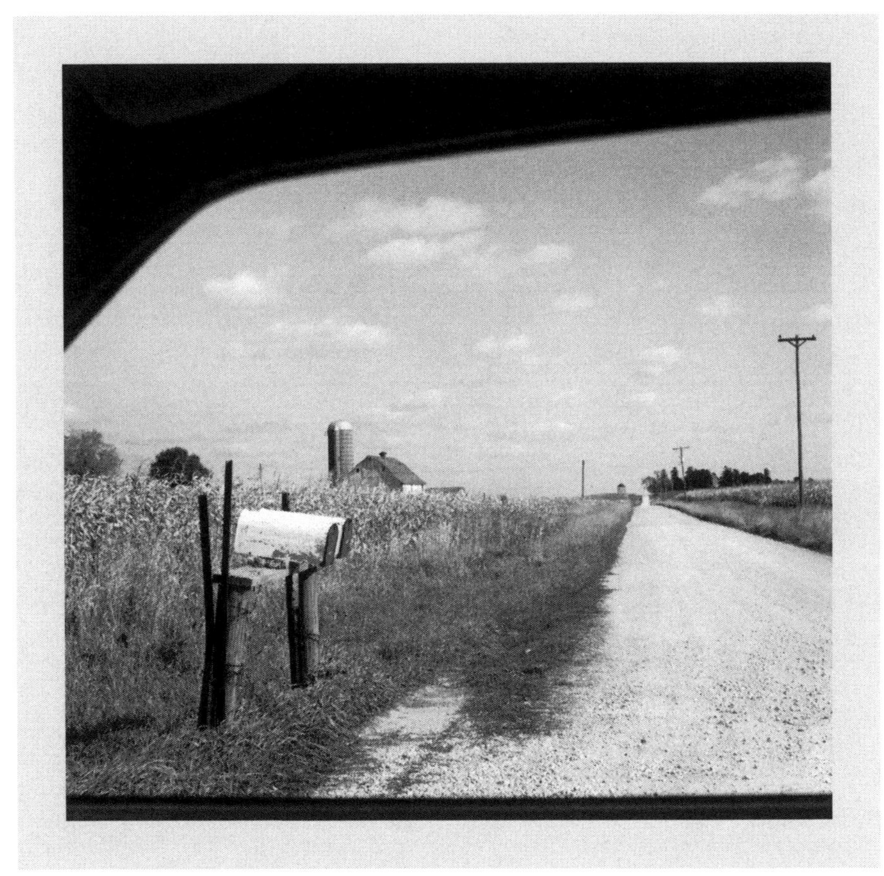

25. House in Ruins on Irene Road

That time of year thou mayst in me behold
When yellow leaves, or none, or few, do hang
Upon those boughs which shake against the cold,
Bare ruin'd choirs where late the sweet birds sang.

William Shakespeare

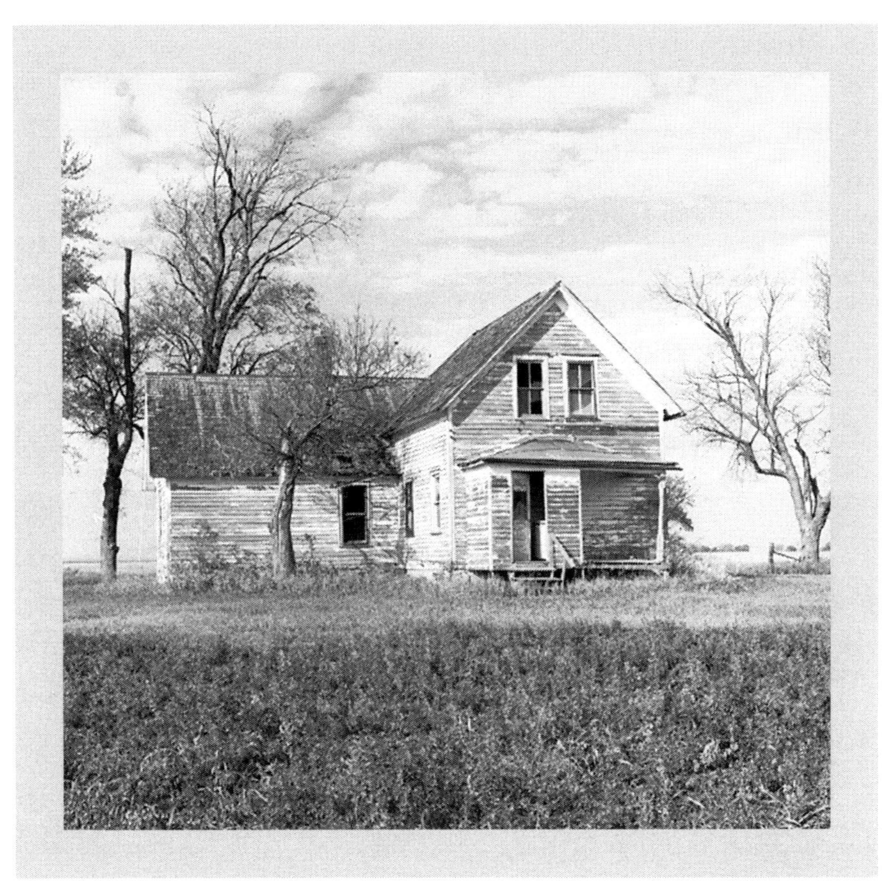

26. Fungi on Tree Trunk at Ellwood House

Stem and leaf grow from it.
At cost of death, it has
A life. Thus falling founds,
Unmaking makes the world.

Wendell Berry

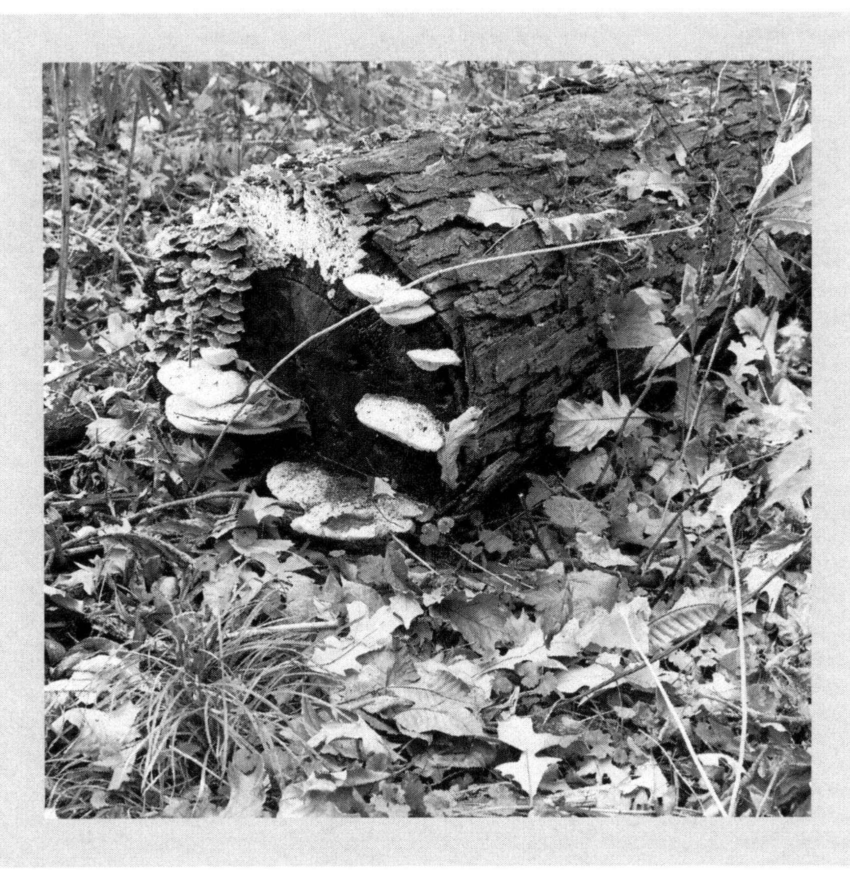

27. Chief Shabbona Forest Preserve

For hundreds of miles no white man lived, but now trading posts and settlers are found here and there throughout the country, and in a few years the smoke from their cabins will be seen to ascend from every grove, and the prairie covered with their cornfields.

Chief Shabbona

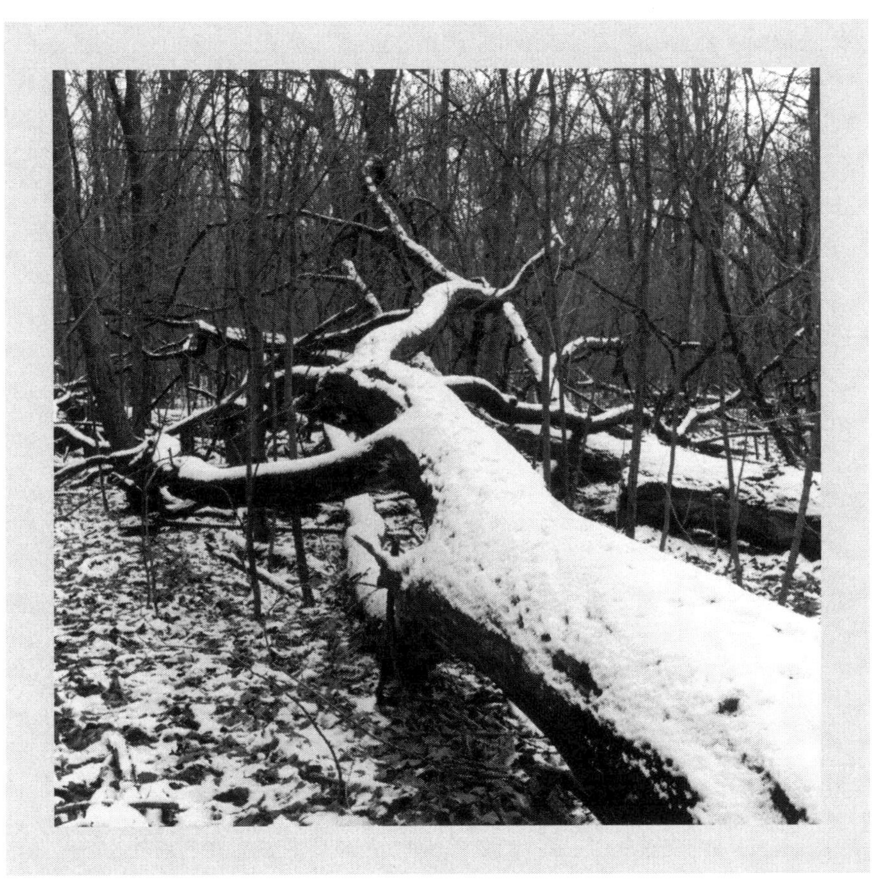

28. Stacks of Shredded Corn Stalks

A mist rose up from the land and moistened the whole face of the earth.

Genesis 2:6

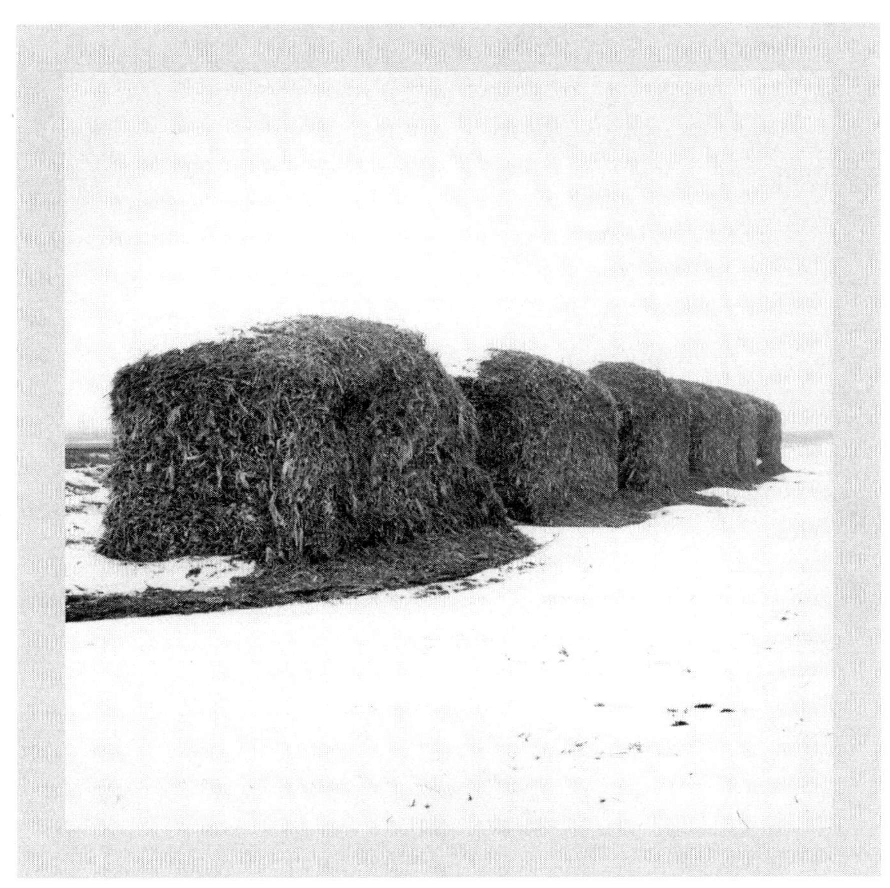

29. Abandoned Farm on Keslinger Road

When we speak of the sublime in nature we speak improperly; properly speaking, sublimity can be attributed merely to our way of thinking.

Immanuel Kant

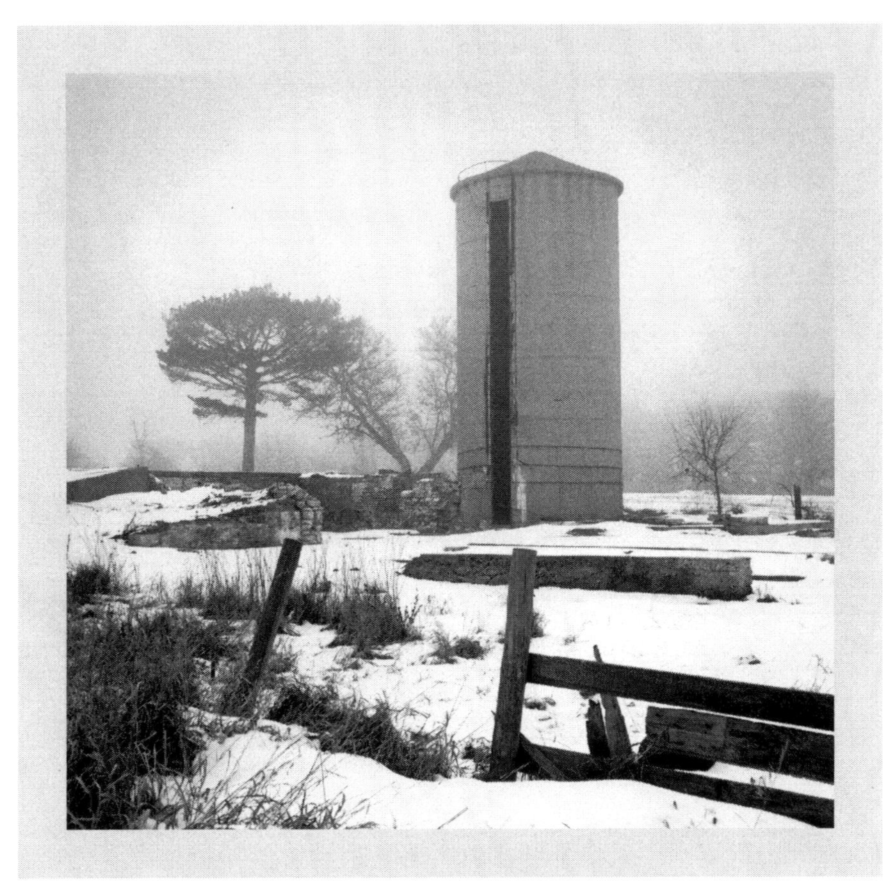

30. Tree Grove in Cornfield

And we, spectators, always, everywhere,
turned toward the world of objects, never outward.
It fills us. We arrange it. It breaks down.
We rearrange it, then break down ourselves.

Rainer Maria Rilke

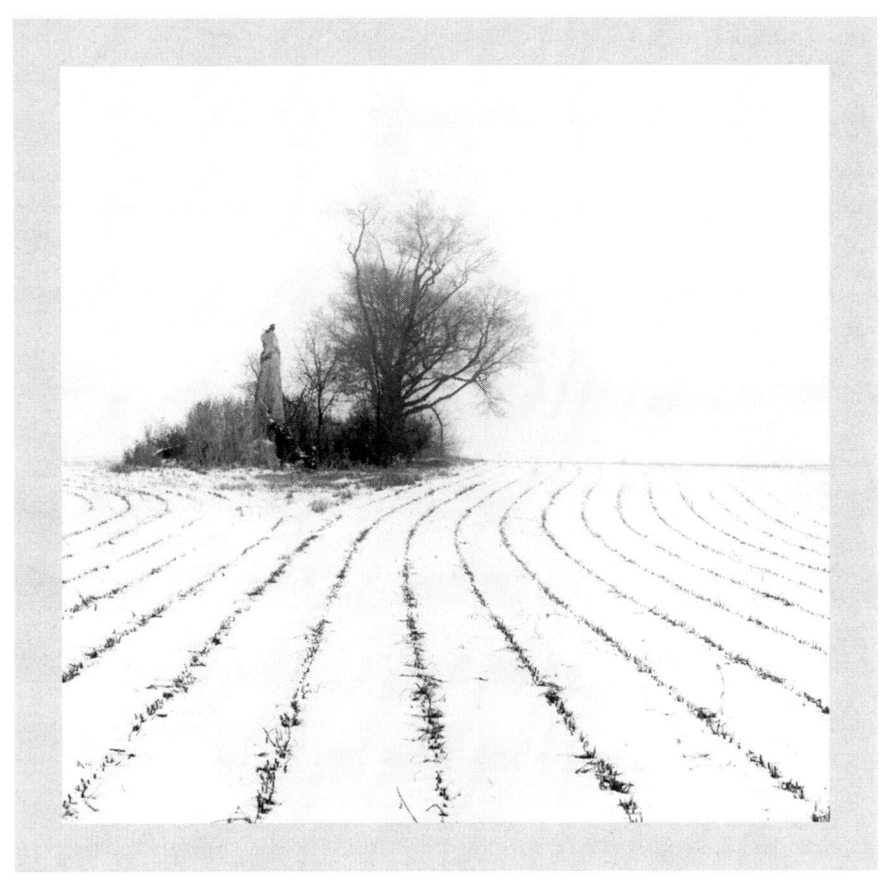

31. Saint Mary's Cemetery on County Line Road

His soul swooned slowly as he heard the snow falling faintly through the universe and faintly falling, like the descent of their last end, upon all the living and the dead.

James Joyce

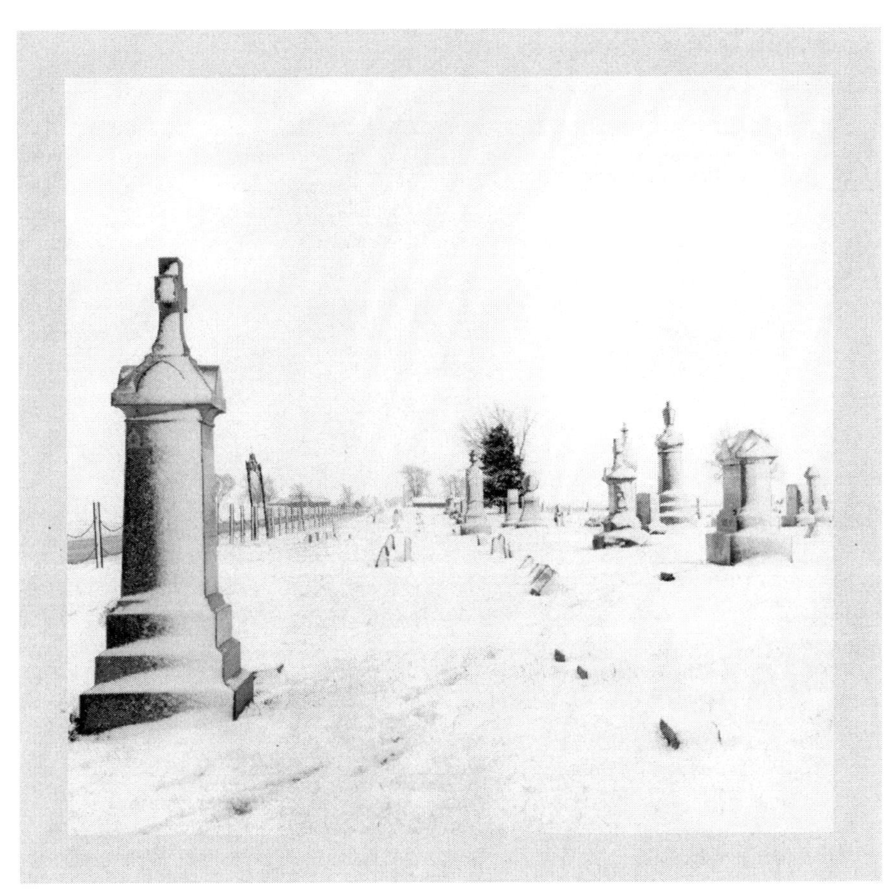

32. White Pines in Lions Park

Be—and yet know the great void where all things begin,
the infinite source of your own most intense vibration
so that, this once, you may give it your perfect assent.

Rainer Maria Rilke

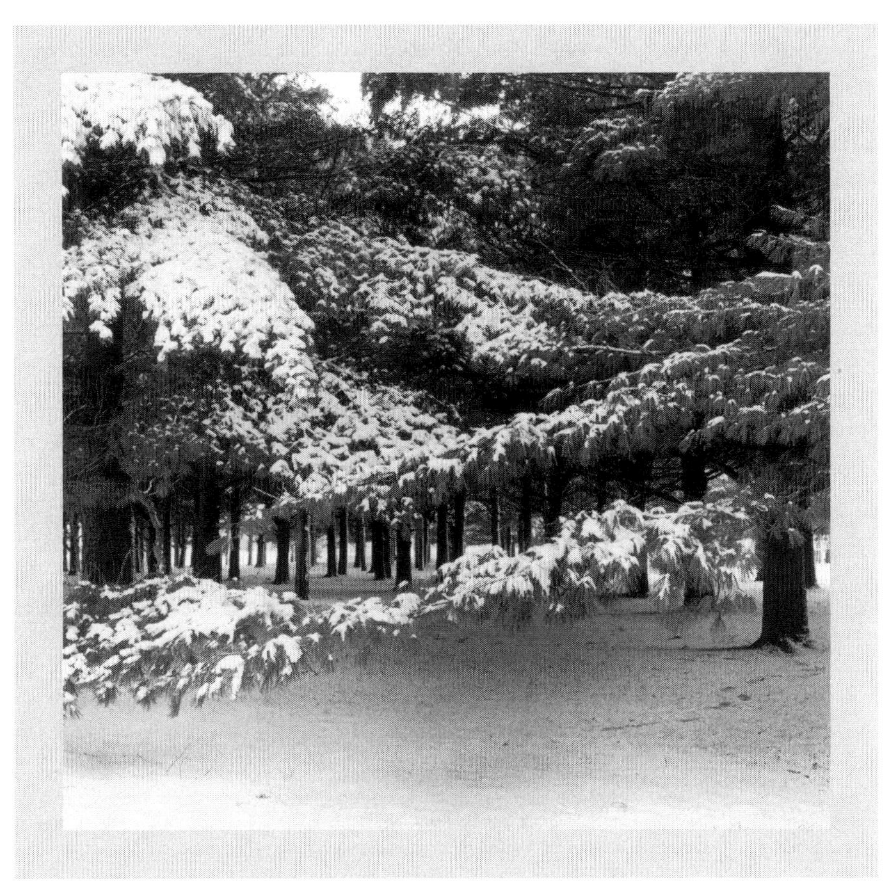

33. Farm Road South of Kingston

I aspire to be as little as possible; that precisely is the core of my melancholy.

Søren Kierkegaard

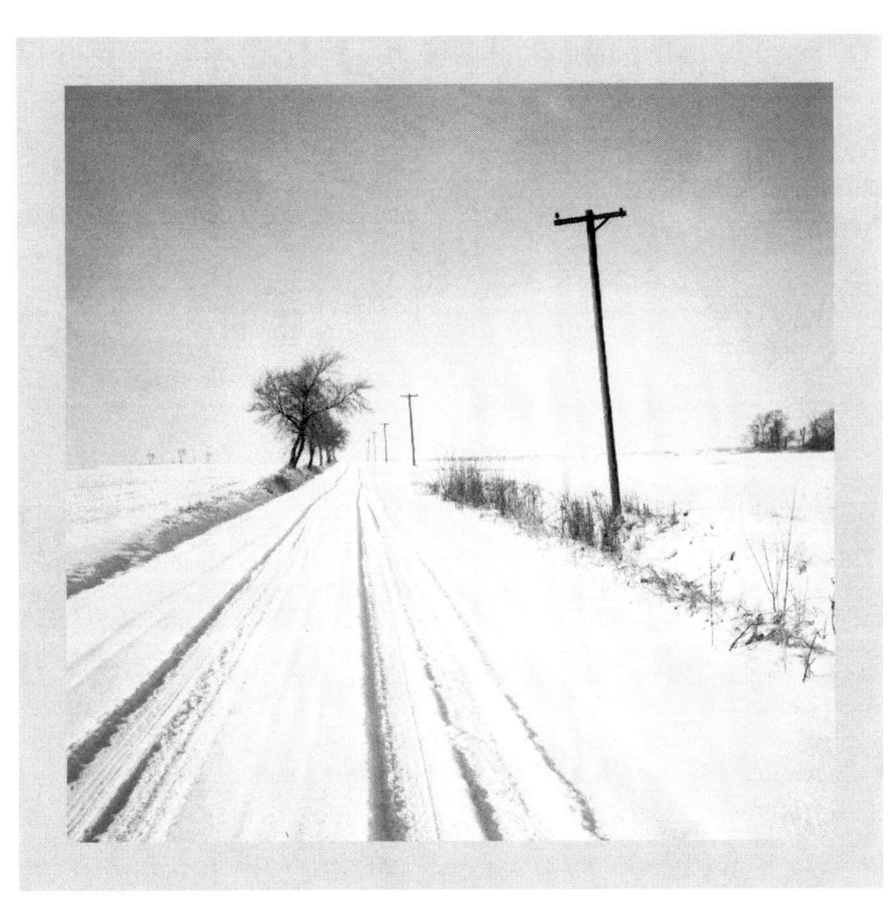

34. Silver Maple Thicket on Five Points Road

You are placed before a thicket. You seek entrance to that which commands your attention. The scene becomes an extension of yourself, a buried meaning, an experience half-remembered, or what you will.

Joseph Leo Koerner

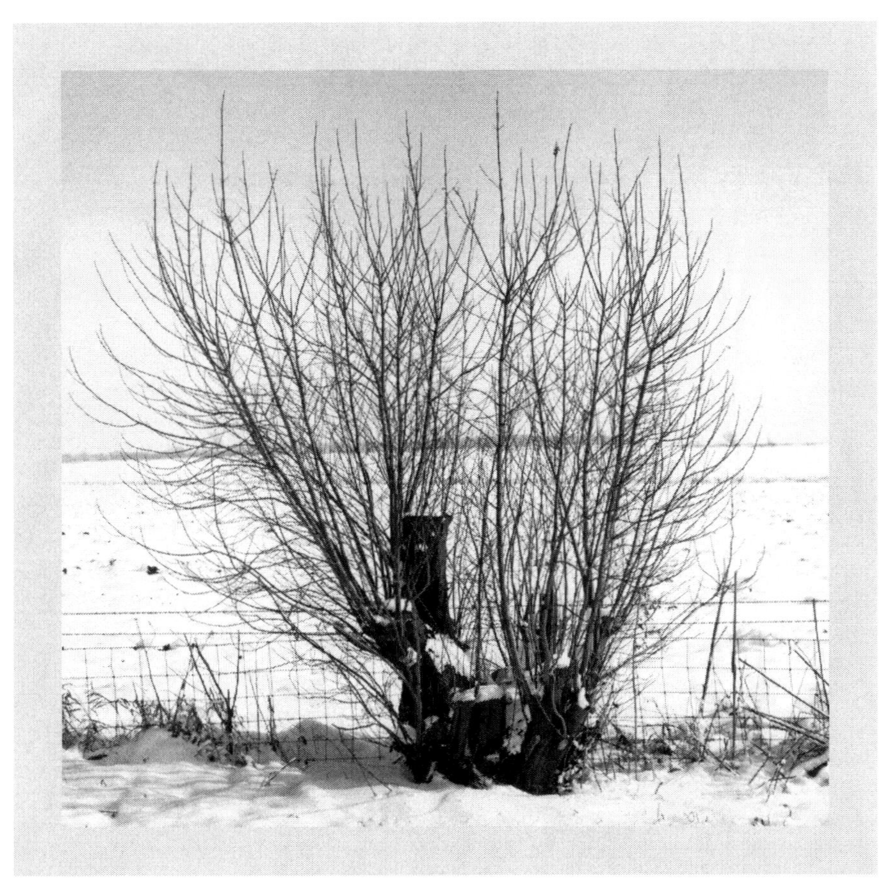

35. **Kishwaukee River North of Town**

The point is that for Harry Callahan photography has been a way of living—his way of meeting and making peace with the day.

John Szarkowski

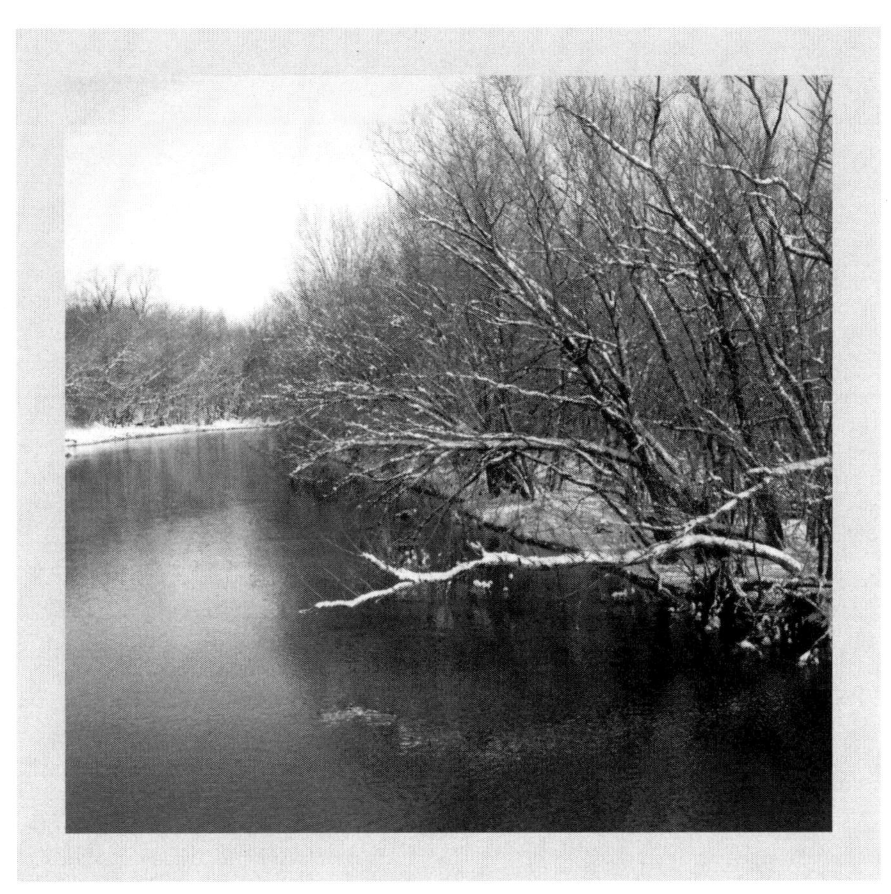

36. **Horse North of Town**

Others say that it was at this time that Jupiter set the winged horse among the stars.

Rex Warner

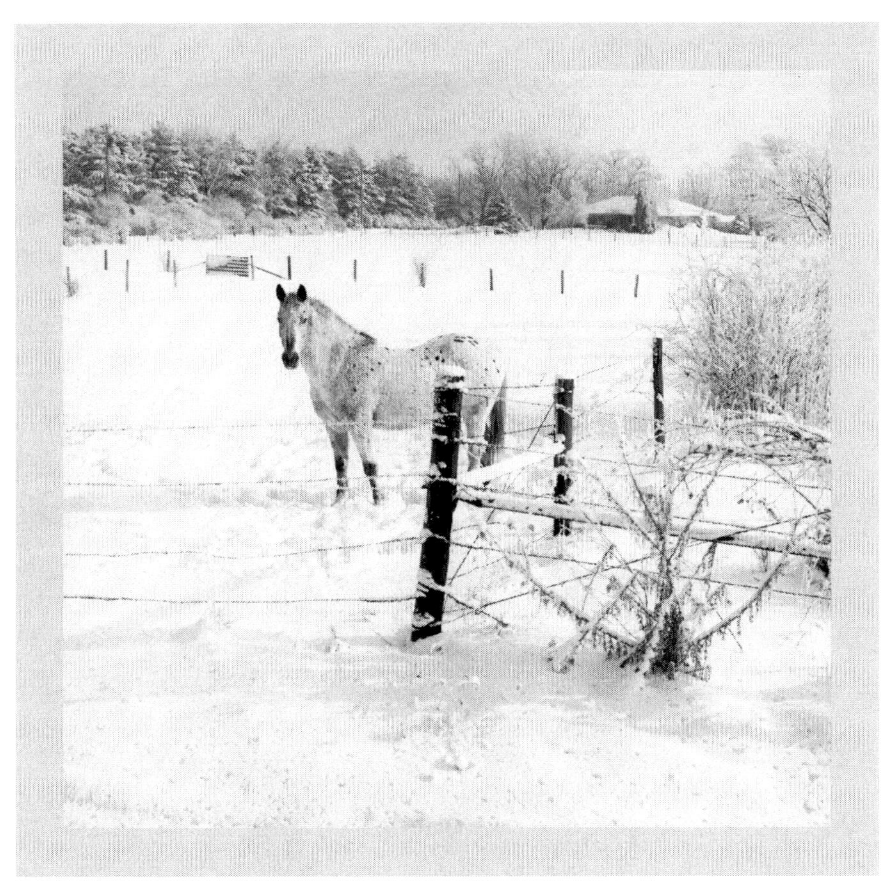

37. **Congregational Church Cemetery**

Arkel: Don't you like the winter?
Melisande: Oh no! I am afraid of the cold. I am so afraid of the great cold.

Maurice Maeterlinck

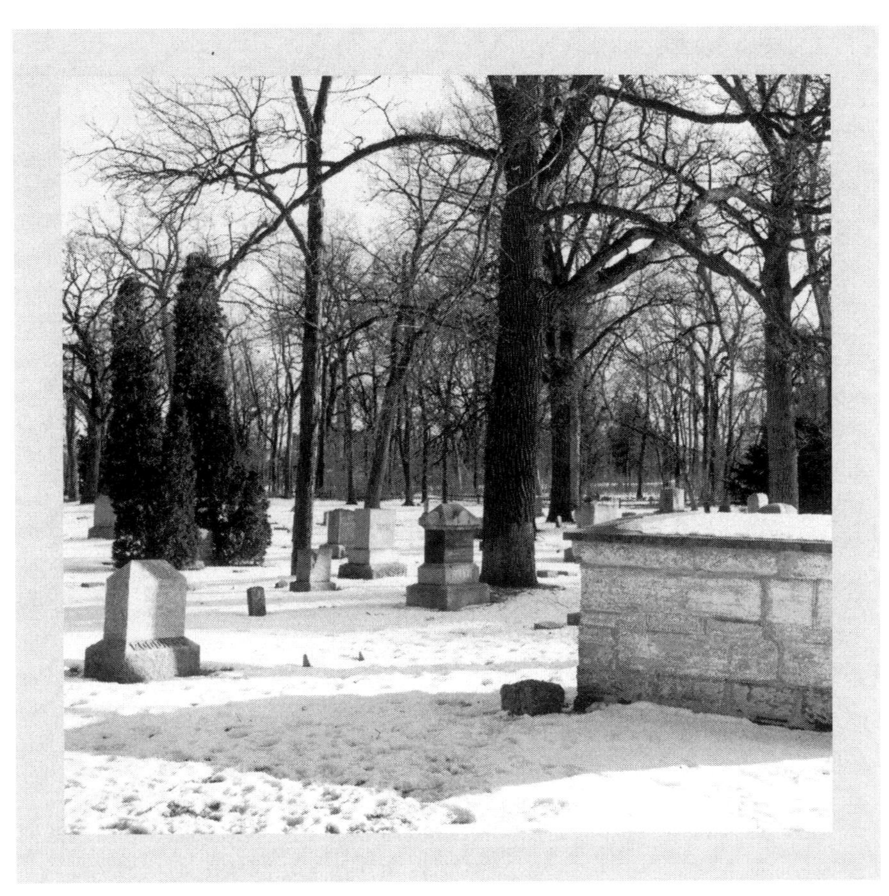

38. **House in Ruins South of Town**

O sweetness of nights where all the stars sway and slide above the masts, and this silence which finally frees me from everything.

Albert Camus

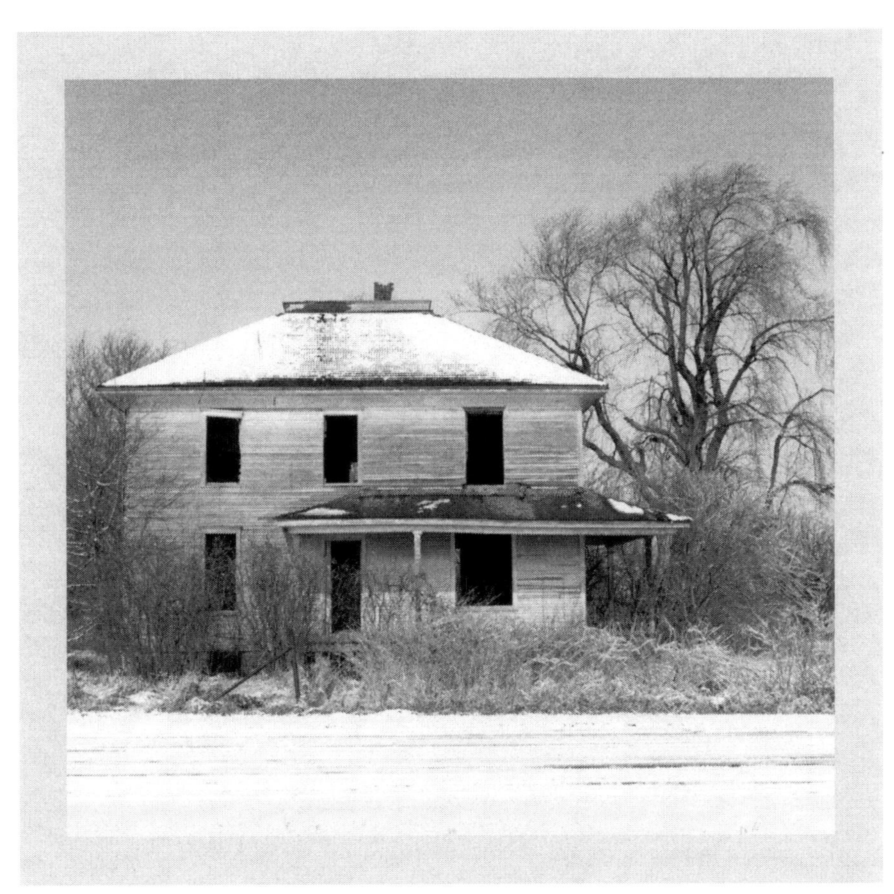

39. **Branch of the Kishwaukee River**

My life consists of the places where I have lived and the work I have accomplished in those places.

Paul Bowles

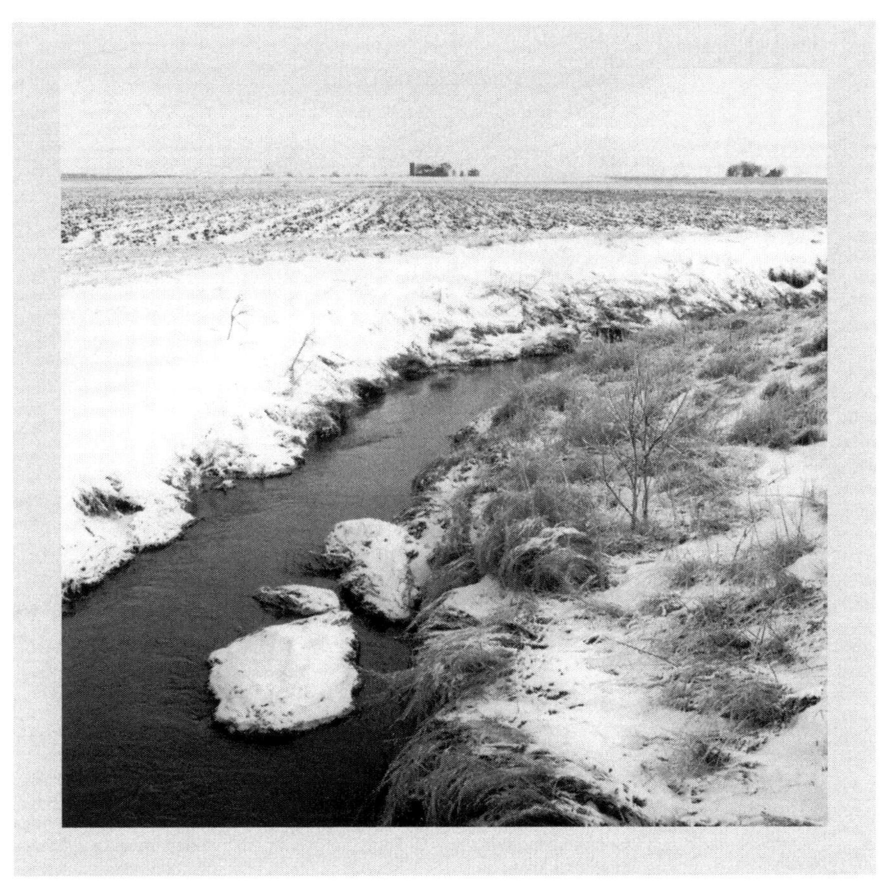

40. **Junkyard in DeKalb**

I'll tell you a big secret, mon cher. Don't wait for the Last Judgment. It takes place every day.

Albert Camus

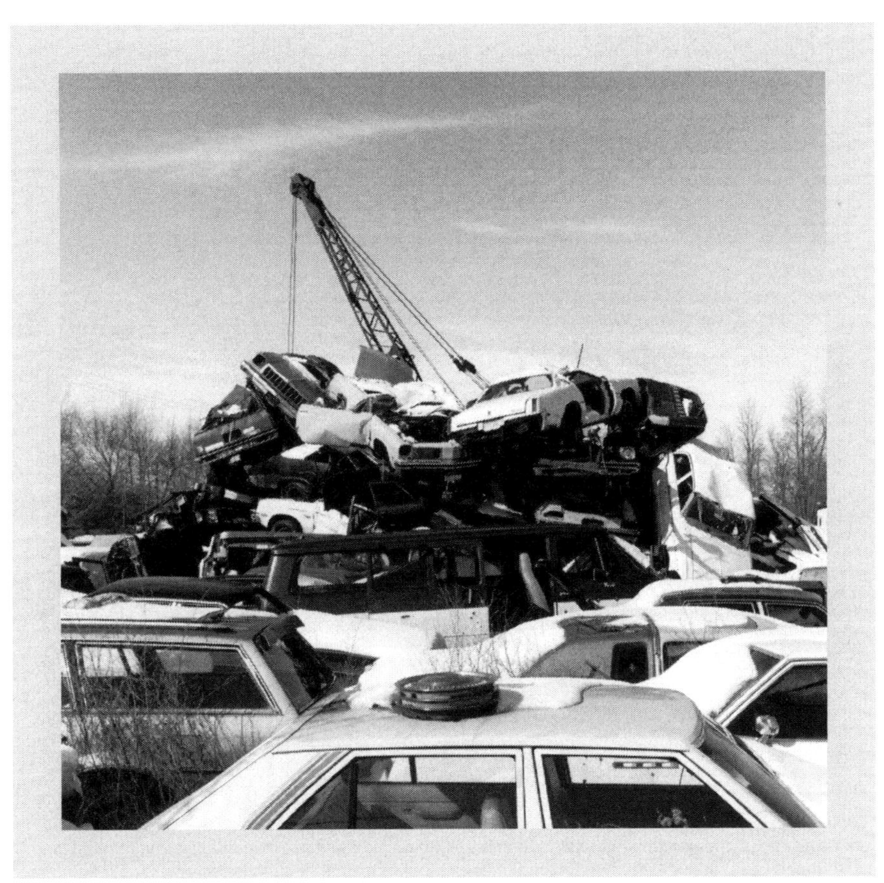

41. Willow Branches

Does it matter? Grace is everywhere...

Georges Bernanos

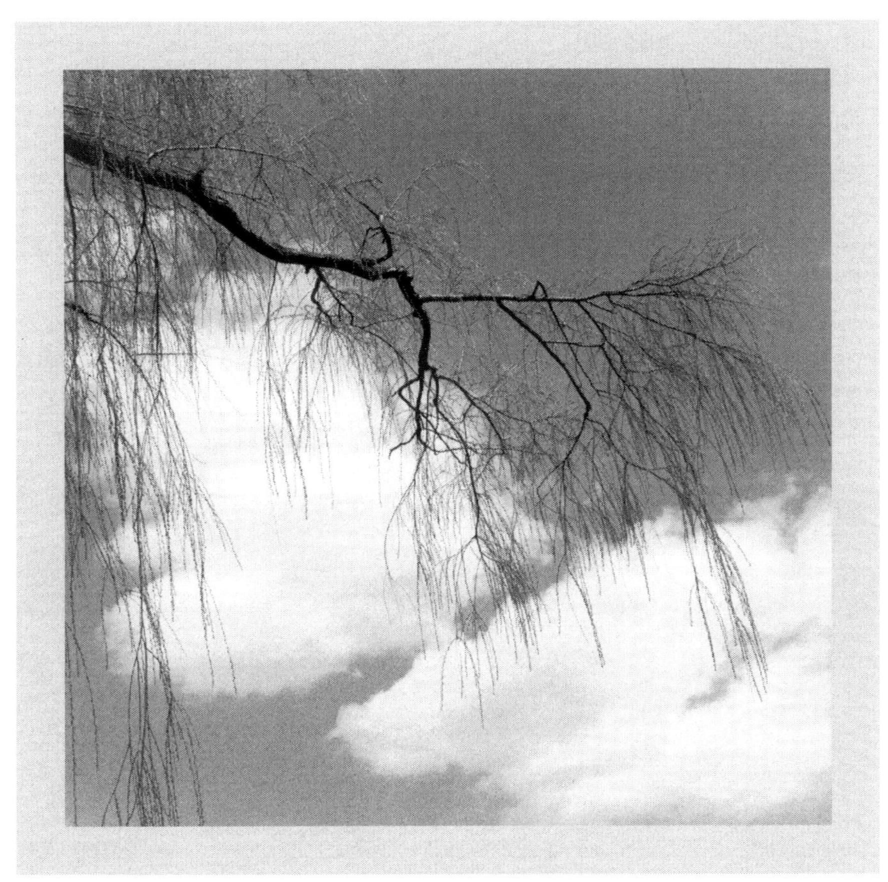

42. DeKalb Cornfest

If you persist in reasoning
About what cannot be understood,
You will be destroyed
By the very thing you seek.

Chuang Tzu

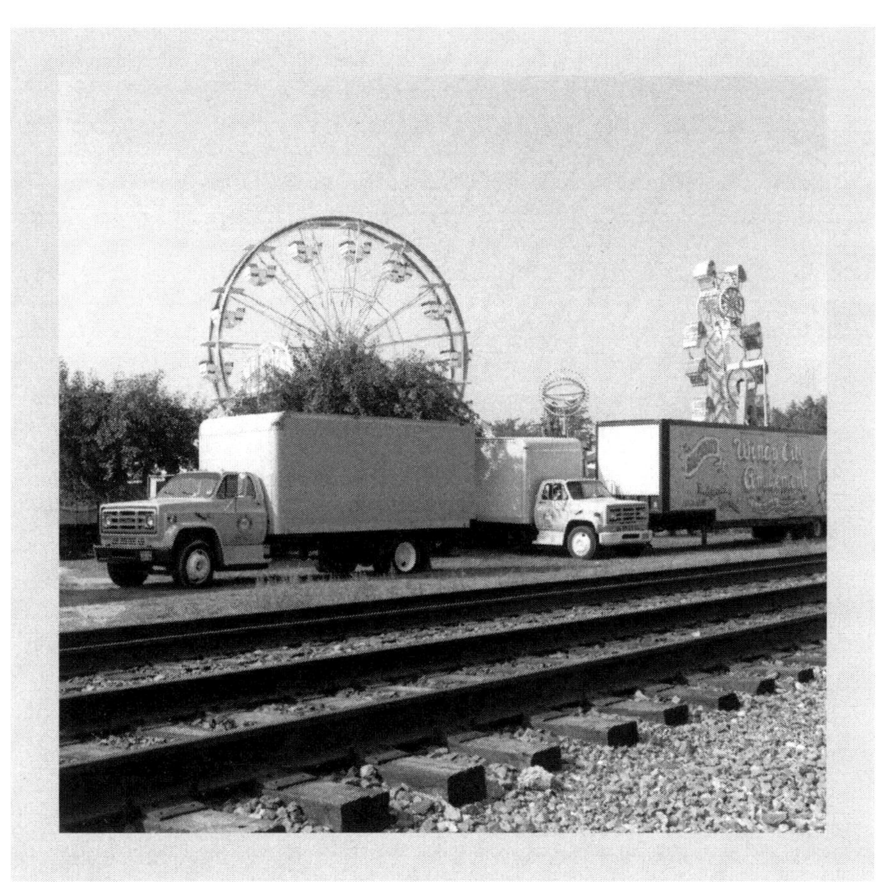

43. Behind East Lincoln Highway

I have to be alone and know that I am alone if I am to examine nature closely and experience her completely. To be what I am, I must devote myself to the world around me, become one with my clouds and cliffs. Solitude is essential to my conversation with nature.

Caspar David Friedrich

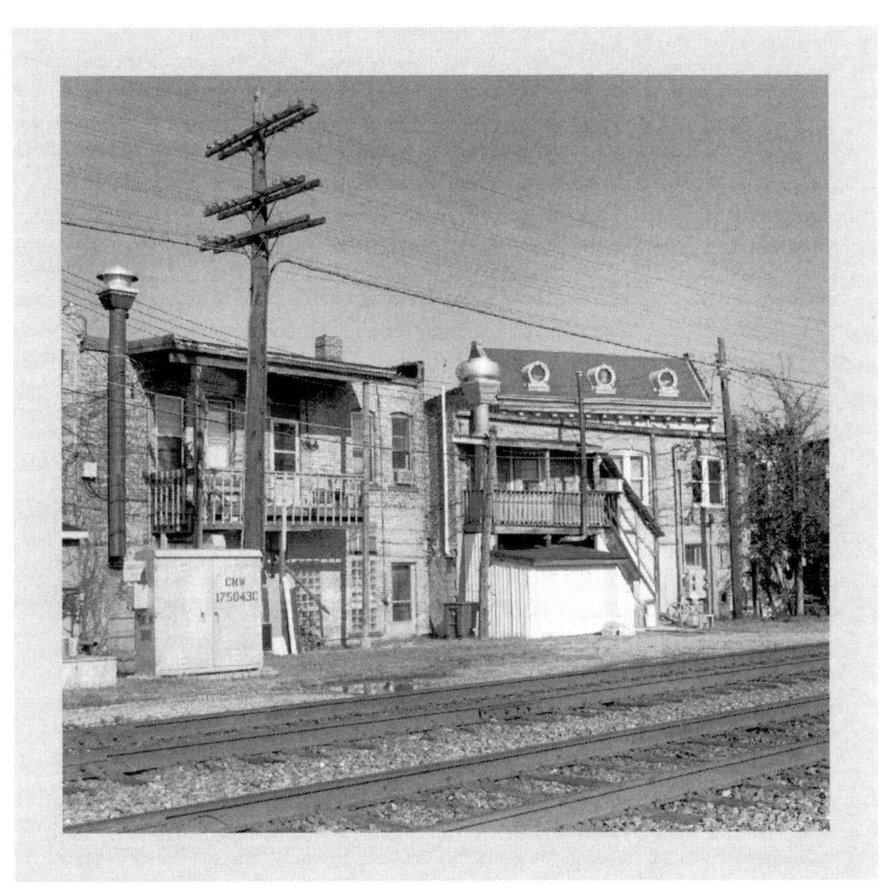
CNW
175043C

44. South Fourth Street

In the pursuit of knowledge,
every day something is added.
In the practice of the Tao,
every day something is dropped.
Less and less do you need to force things,
until finally you arrive at non-action.
When nothing is done,
nothing is left undone.

Lao-tzu

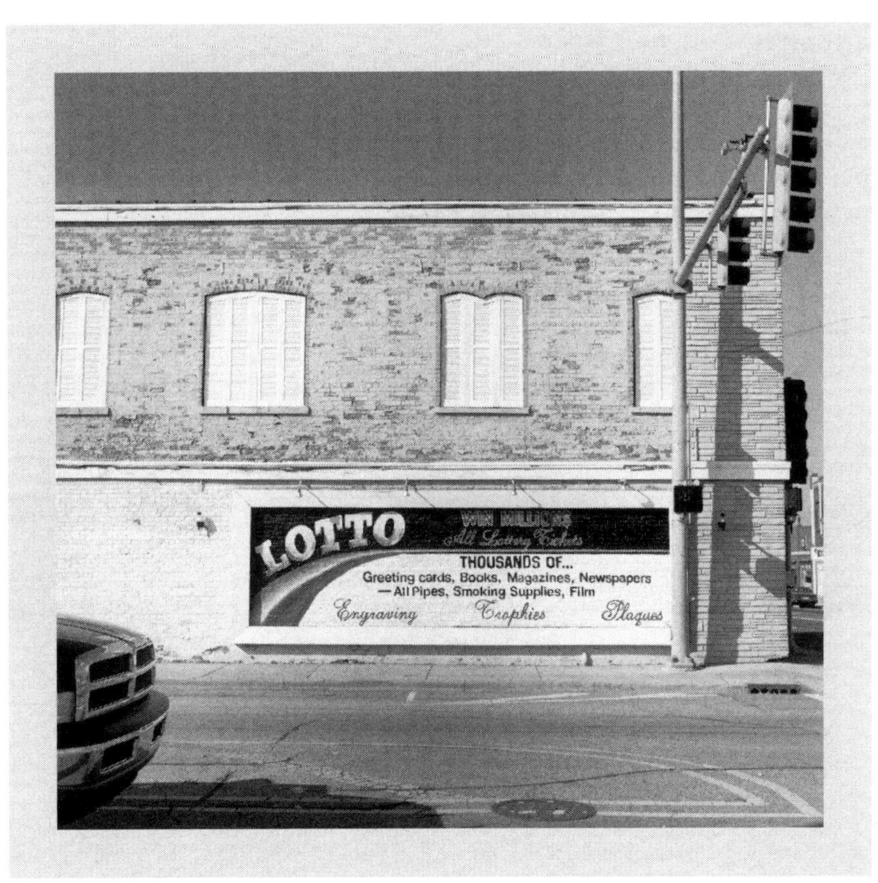
LOTTO
THOUSANDS OF...
Greeting cards, Books, Magazines, Newspapers
— All Pipes, Smoking Supplies, Film
Engraving
Trophies
Plaques

45. **Hintzsche Fertilizer**

Everything exists, everything is true, and the earth is only a little dust under our feet.

W. B. Yeats

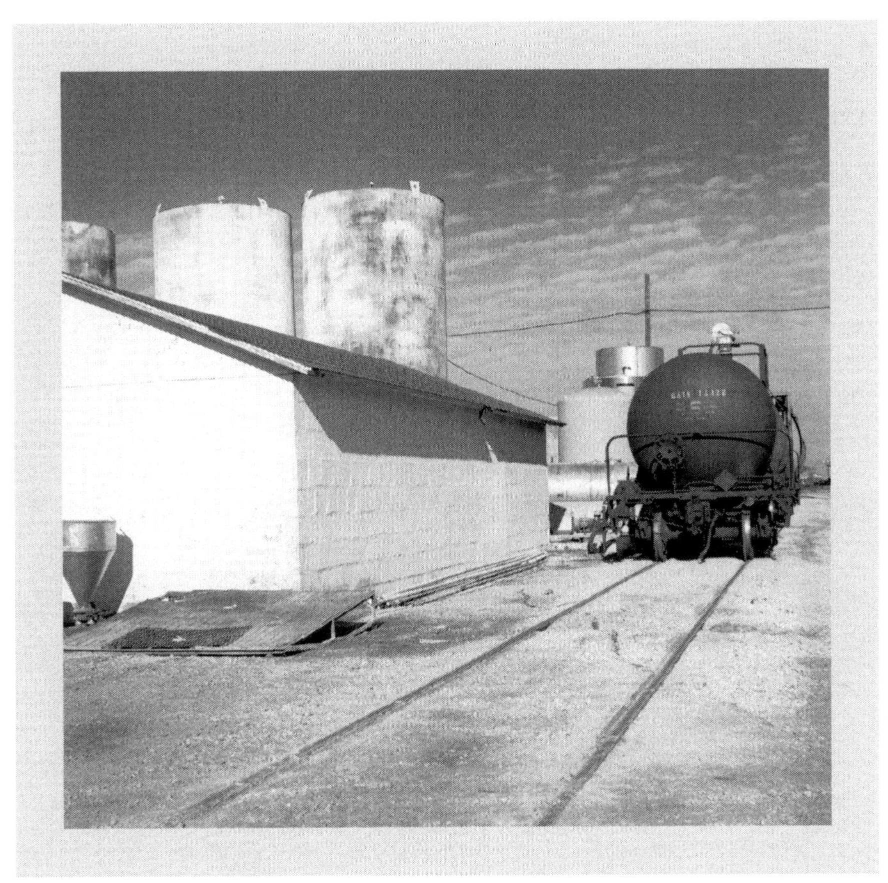

46. **East Lagoon in Winter**

We shall not cease from exploration
And the end of all our exploring
Will be to arrive where we started
And know the place for the first time.

T. S. Eliot

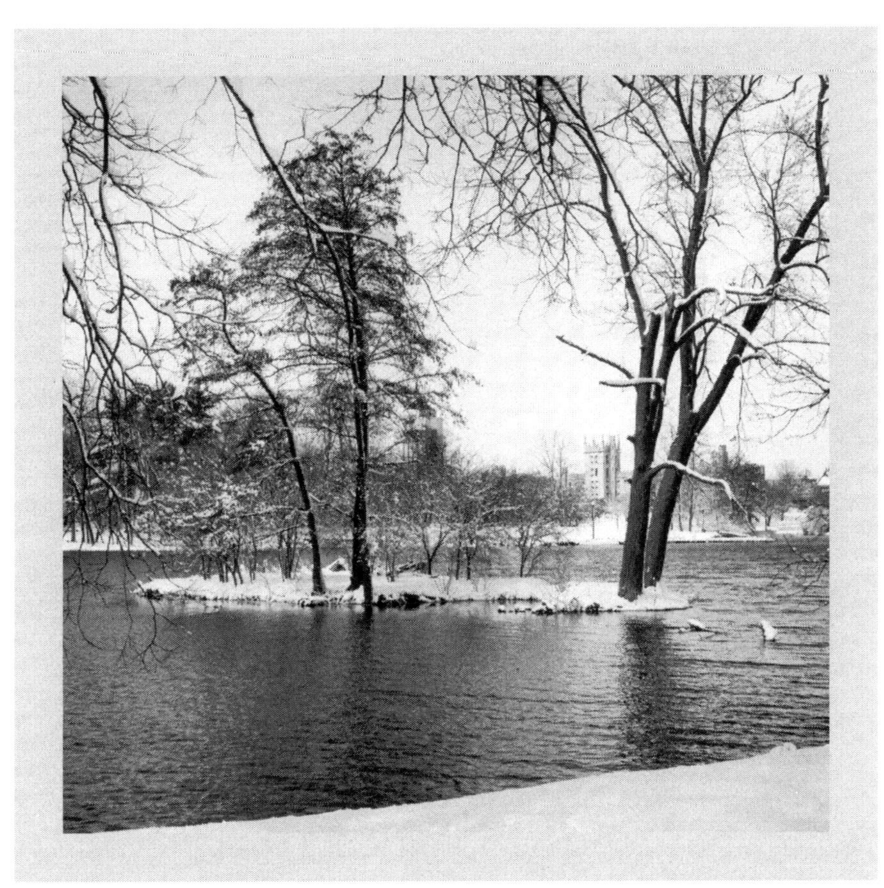

47. **Winter Storage**

There is so little to say, and so much time to say it in.

Charles Wright

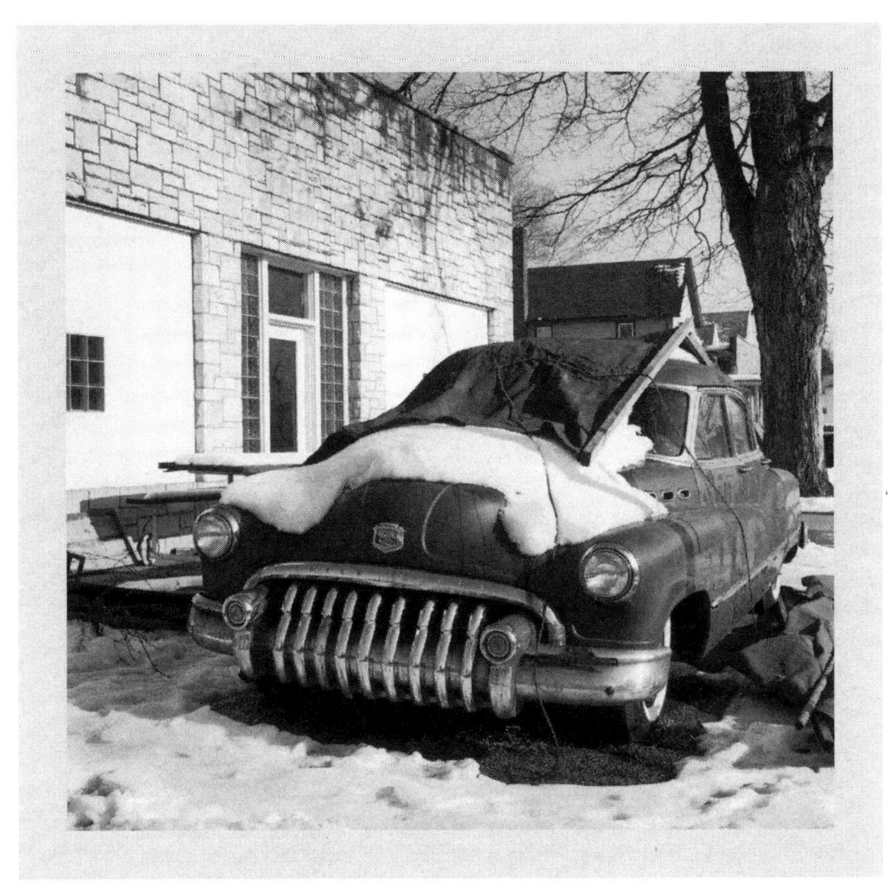

48. Coal Chute in Town

All things have the nature of mind. Mind is the chief and takes the lead. If the mind is clear, whatever you do or say will bring happiness that will follow you like your shadow.

The Dhammapada

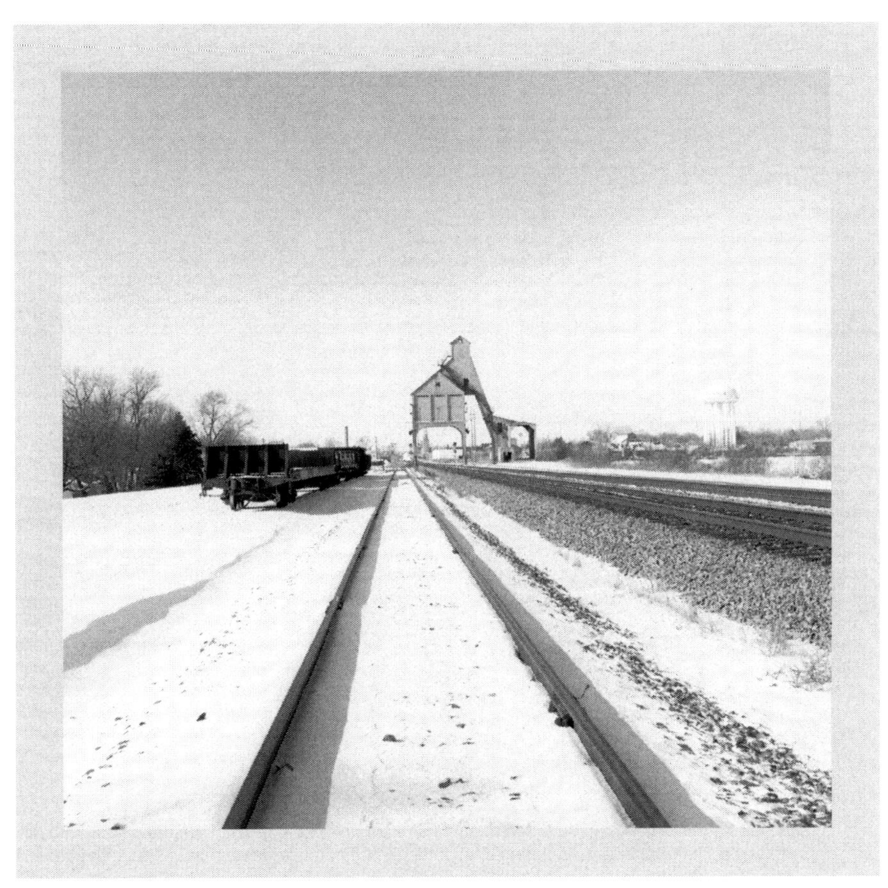

49. **Sullivan's Tavern**

A day will come when some laborious monk
Will bring to light my zealous, nameless toil,
Kindle, as I, his lamp, and from the parchment
Shaking the dust of ages will transcribe
My true narrations.

Alexander Pushkin

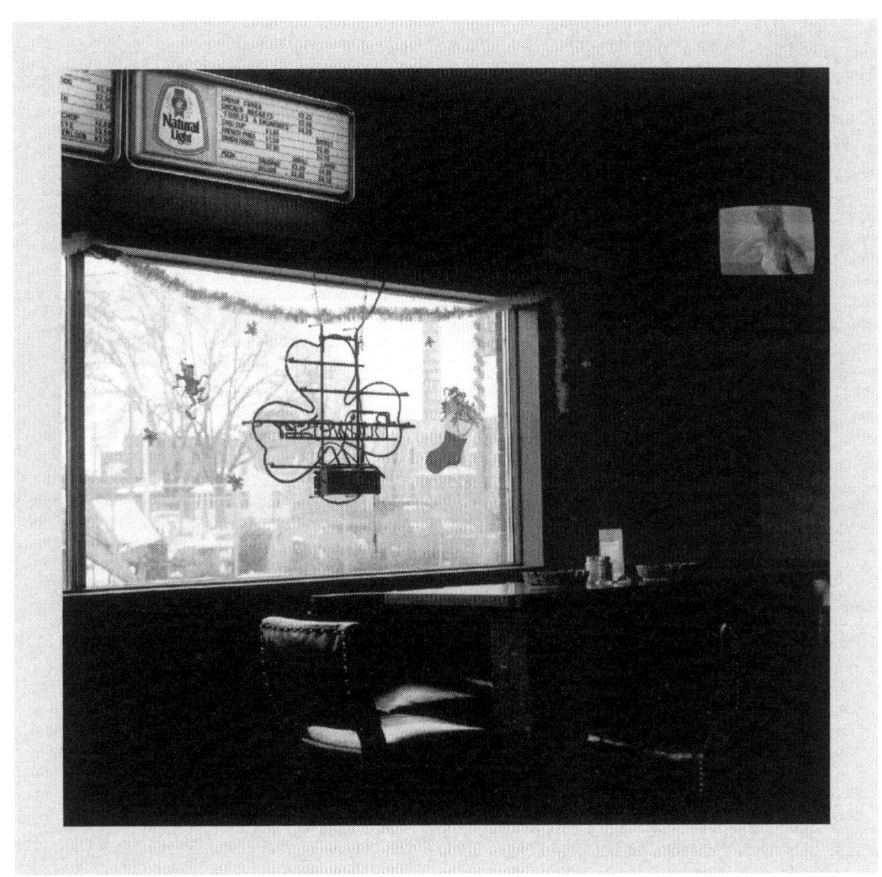
Natural Light

50. Oak Tree in the Congregational Cemetery

I look for my old friend. He is nowhere.
Only the Han River flowing daily into the east.
I might ask for the old man of Xiangyang
but among mountains and rivers his Caizhou island
  is today desolate.

Wang Wei

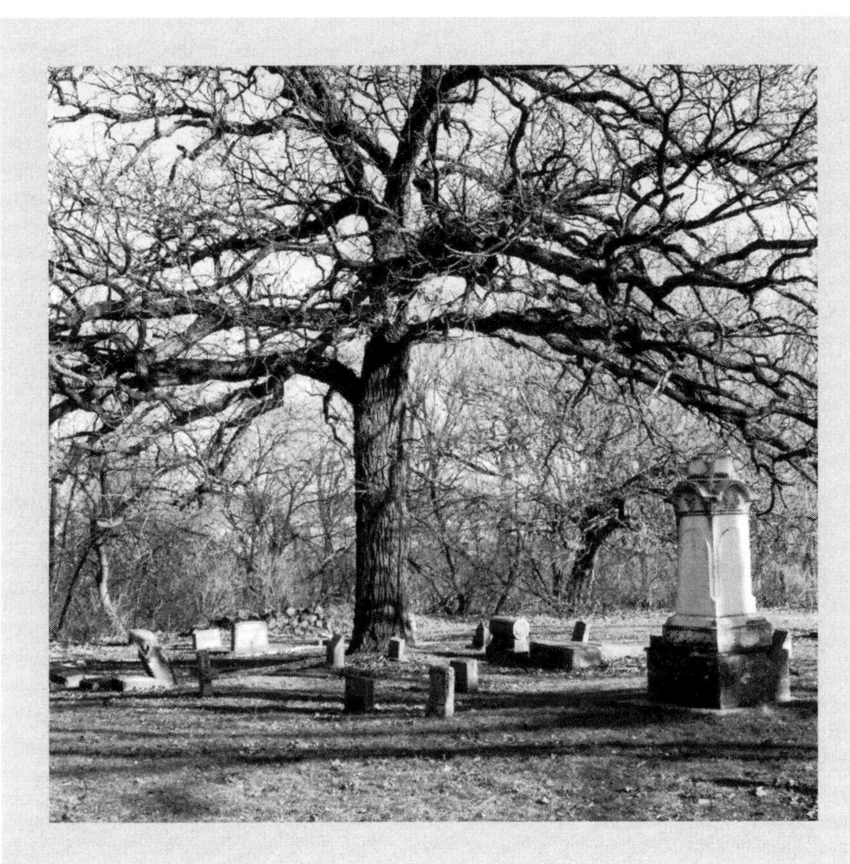

51. Train Speeding through Town

I heard that lonesome whistle blow.

Jimmie Davis and Hank Williams

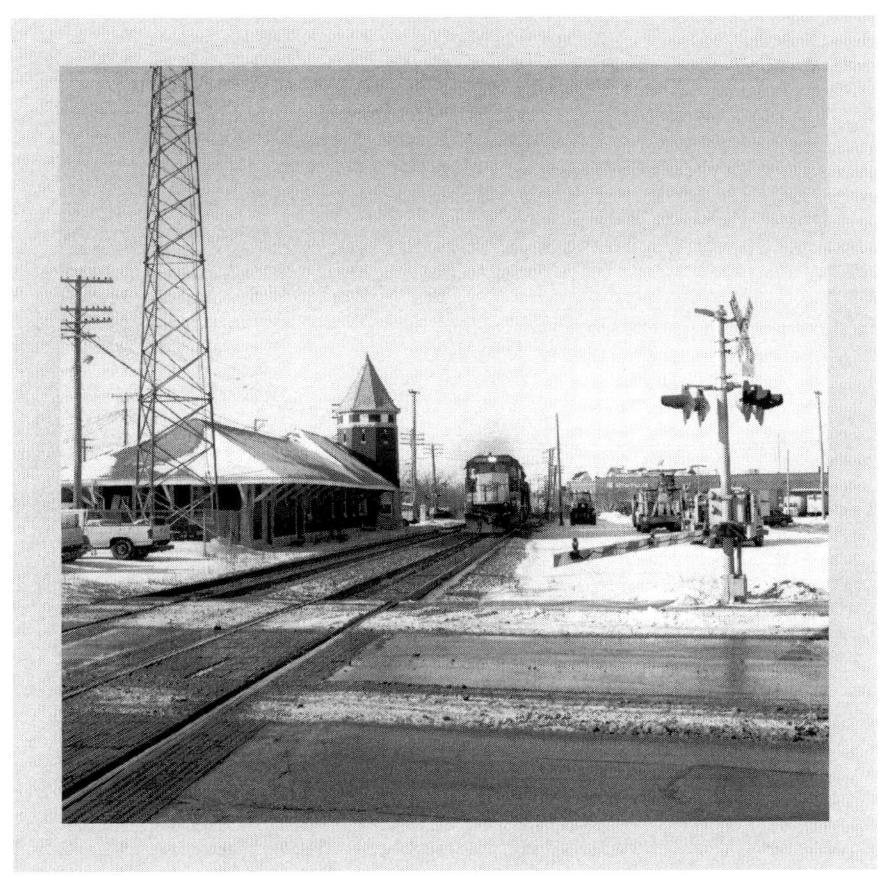

52. Bird Nest at Home

We all dwell in a house of one room—the world with the firmament for its roof—and are sailing the celestial spaces without leaving any track.

John Muir

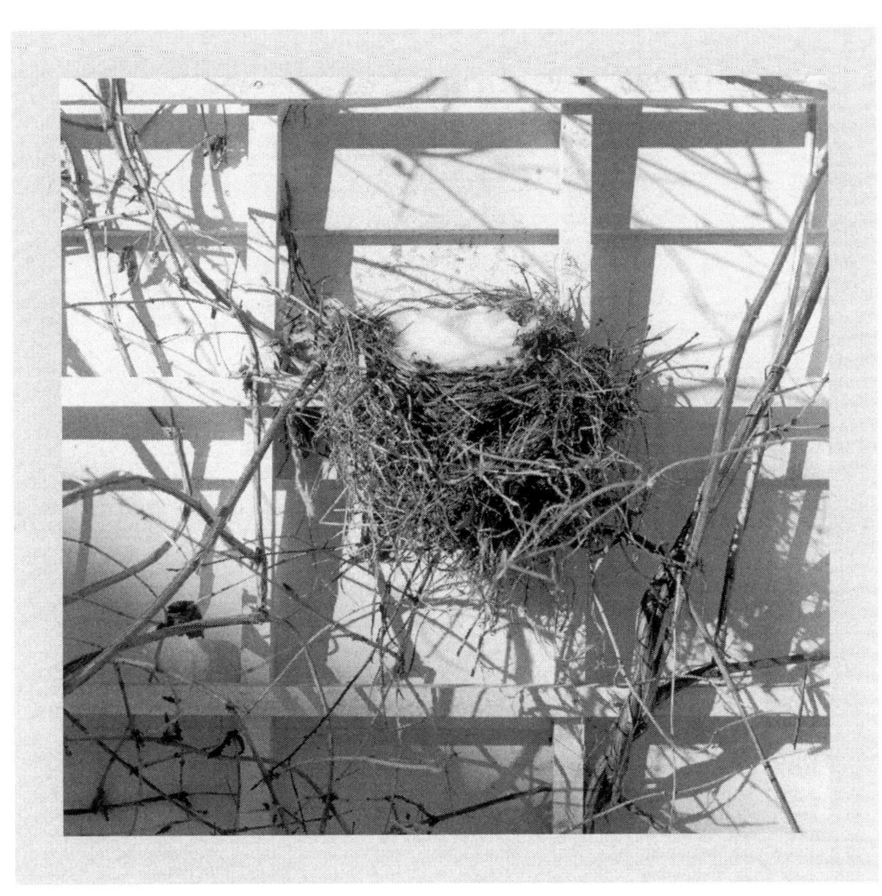

53. Old Post Office Building

I considered my handiwork, all of my labor and toil: it was futility, all of it, and a chasing of the wind, of no profit under the sun.

Ecclesiastes 2:11

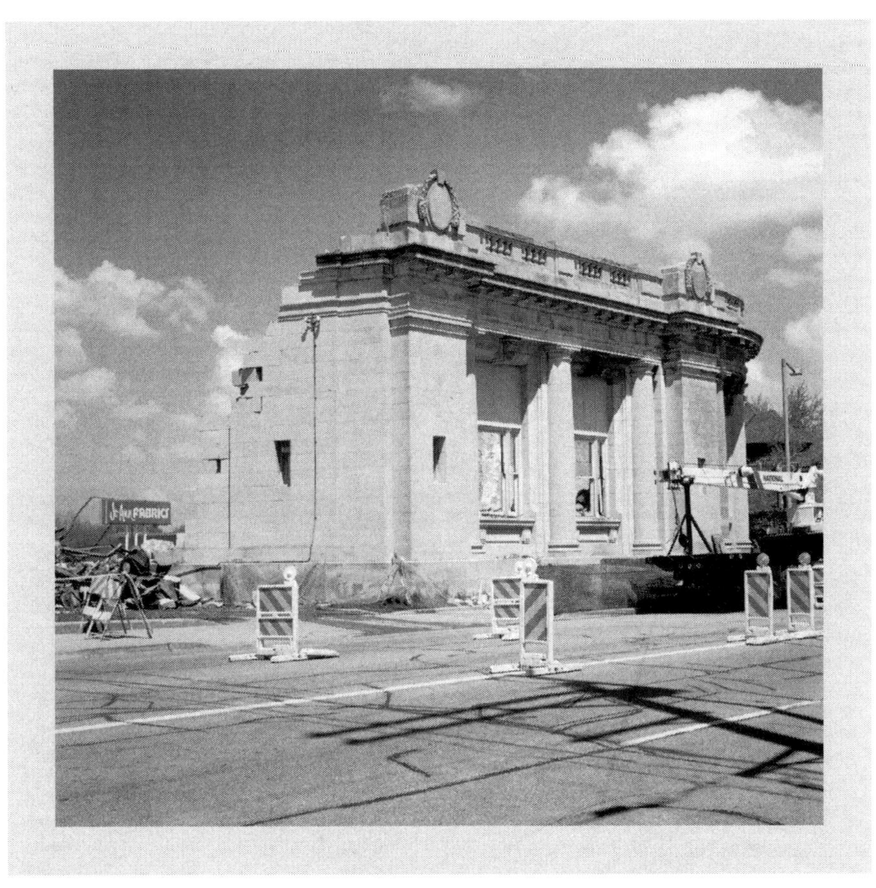
FABRICS

54. Entering DeKalb from Chicago

I can't stay. I can't go. Let's see what happens next.

Samuel Beckett

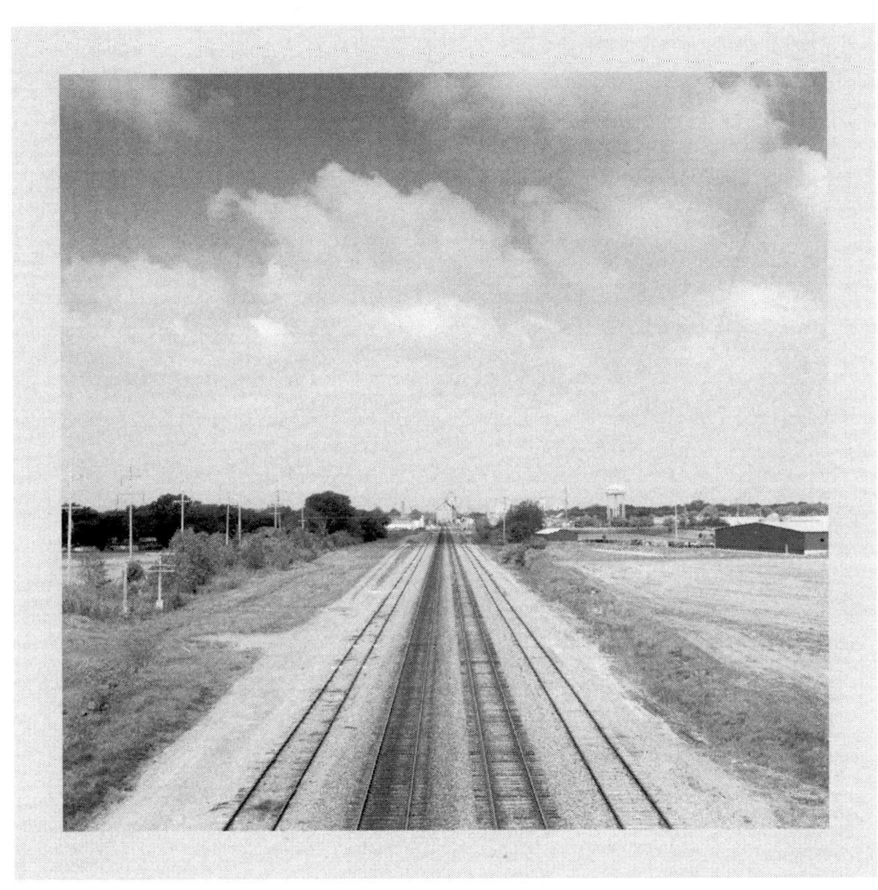

55. Willow Branches at the Lagoon in Winter

If you want life, do not cling to it, let it go.

Alan Watts

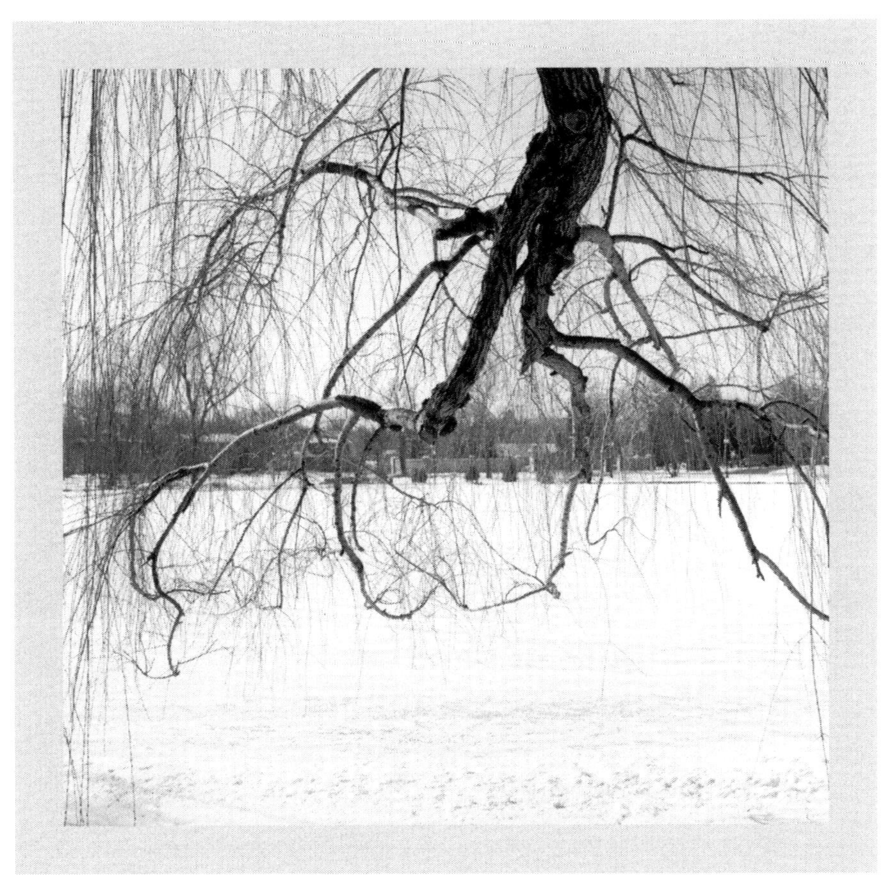

56. Still Life at Home

If you take photography seriously you must also get interested in another art form. For me it is music. This listening to music shows up in my work like a reflection in a mirror. I relax and the world looks less unpleasant, and I can see that all around there is beauty, such as music.

Josef Sudek

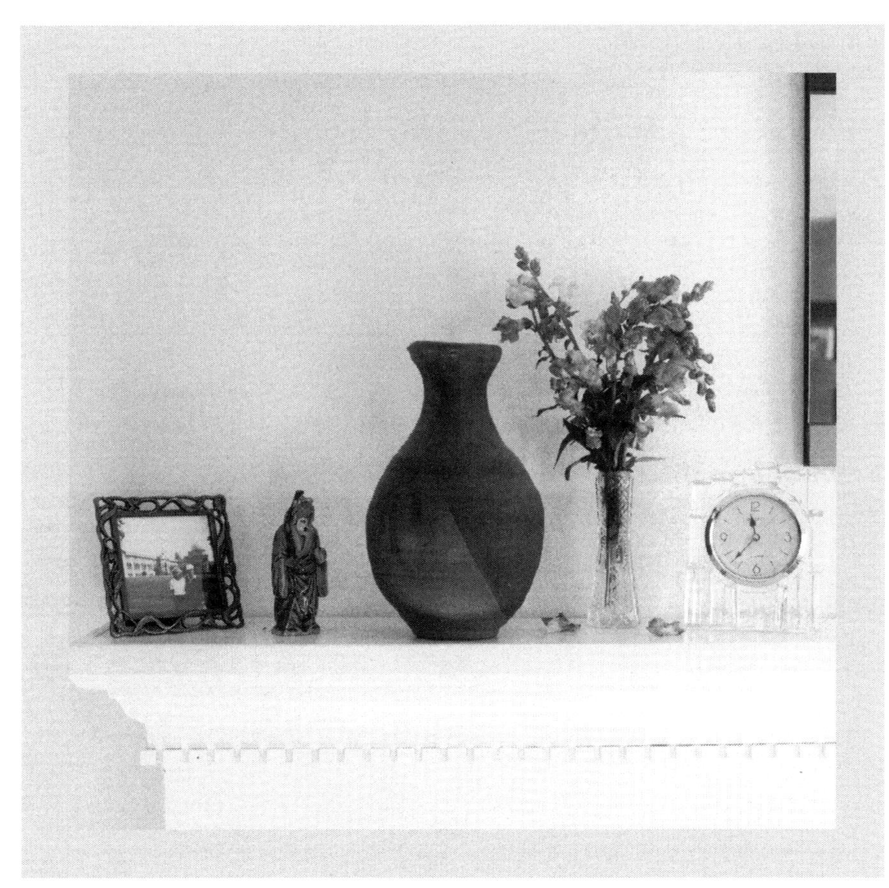

57. Bedroom

Wait without thought, for you are not ready for thought:
So the darkness shall be the light, and the stillness the dancing.

T. S. Eliot

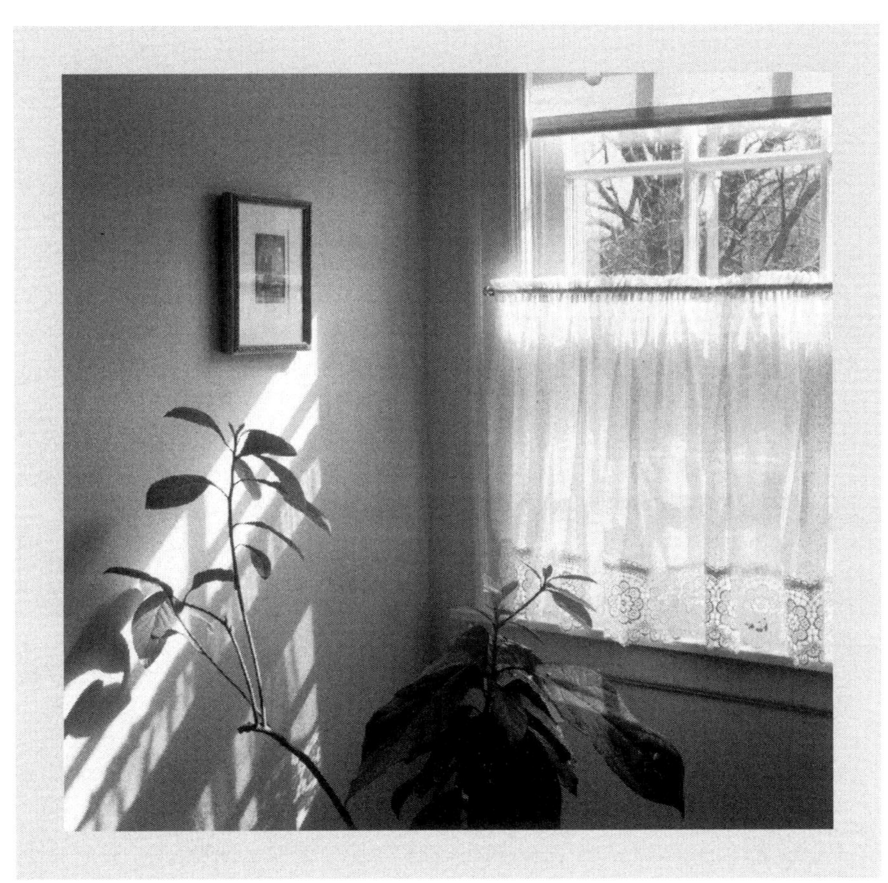

58. Kishwaukee River at the End of the Street

One day you will be one of those who lived long ago.
The earth will remember you just as it remembers the grass
and the woods,
the rotting leaves.
Just as the soil remembers
and just as the mountains remember the winds.
Your peace shall be as unending as the sea.

Pär Lagerkvist

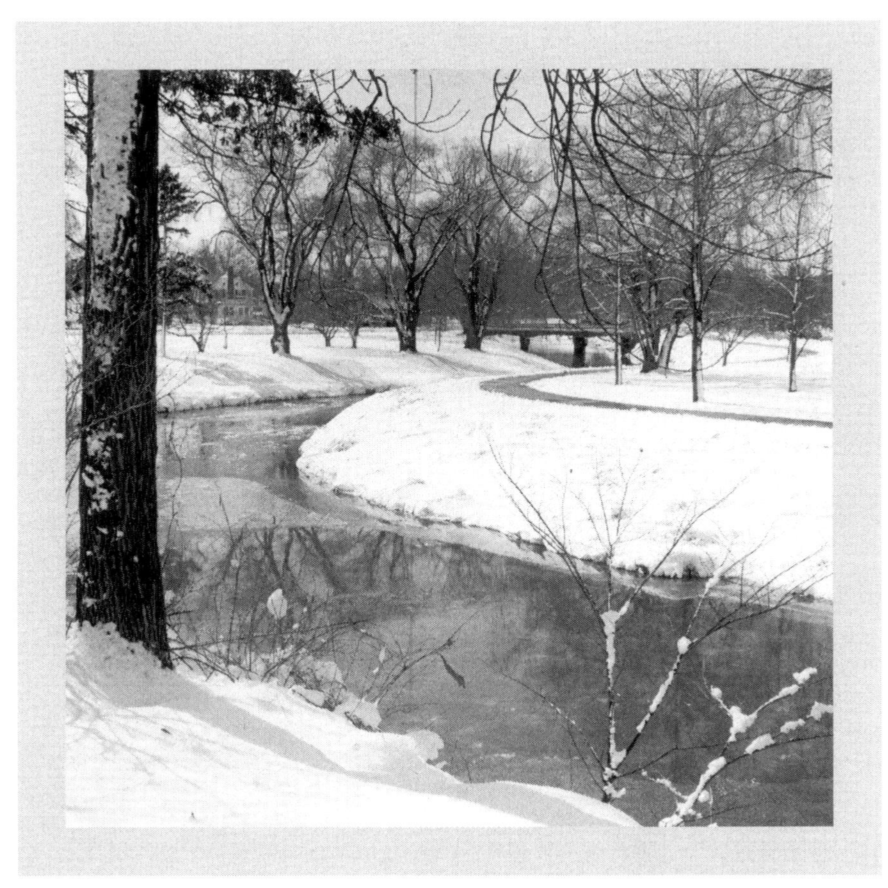

59. Bridge over the East Lagoon

My hut lies in the middle of a dense forest;
Every year the green ivy grows longer.
No news of the affairs of men,
Only the occasional song of a woodcutter.
The sun shines and I mend my robe;
When the moon comes out I read Buddhist poems.
I have nothing to report, my friends.
If you want to find the meaning, stop chasing after
so many things.

Ryōkan

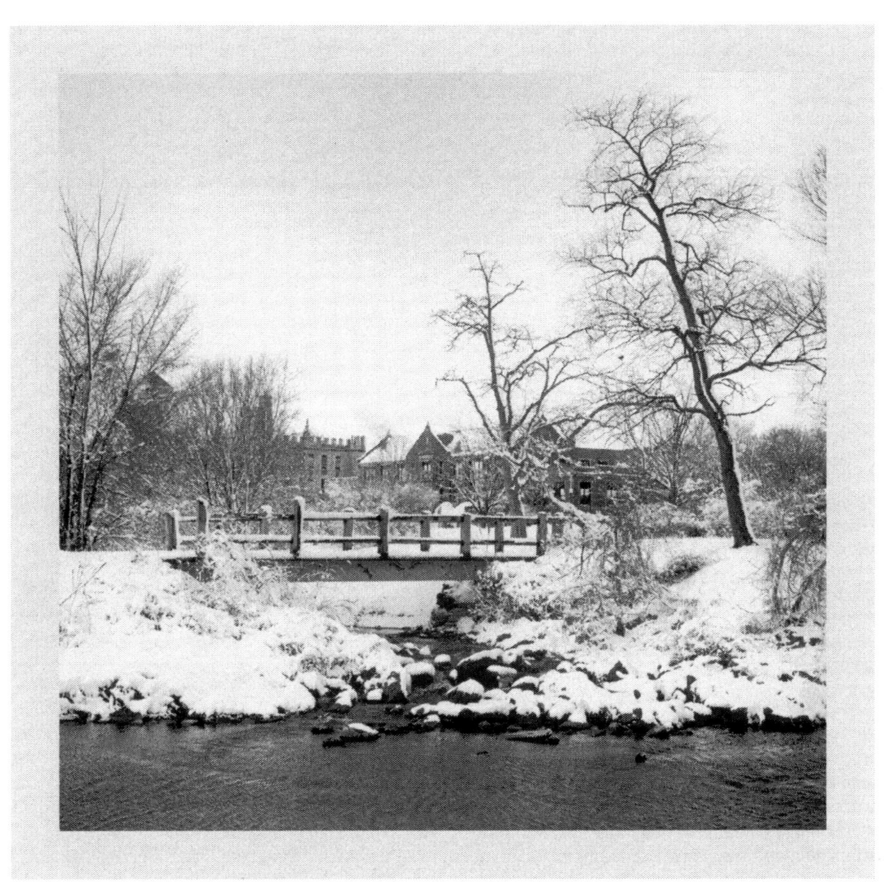

60. **Illinois Central Tracks North of Town**

When we are deeply in touch with the present moment, we can see that all our ancestors and all future generations are present in us. Seeing this, we will know what to do and what not to do for ourselves, our ancestors, our children, and their children.

Thich Nhat Hanh

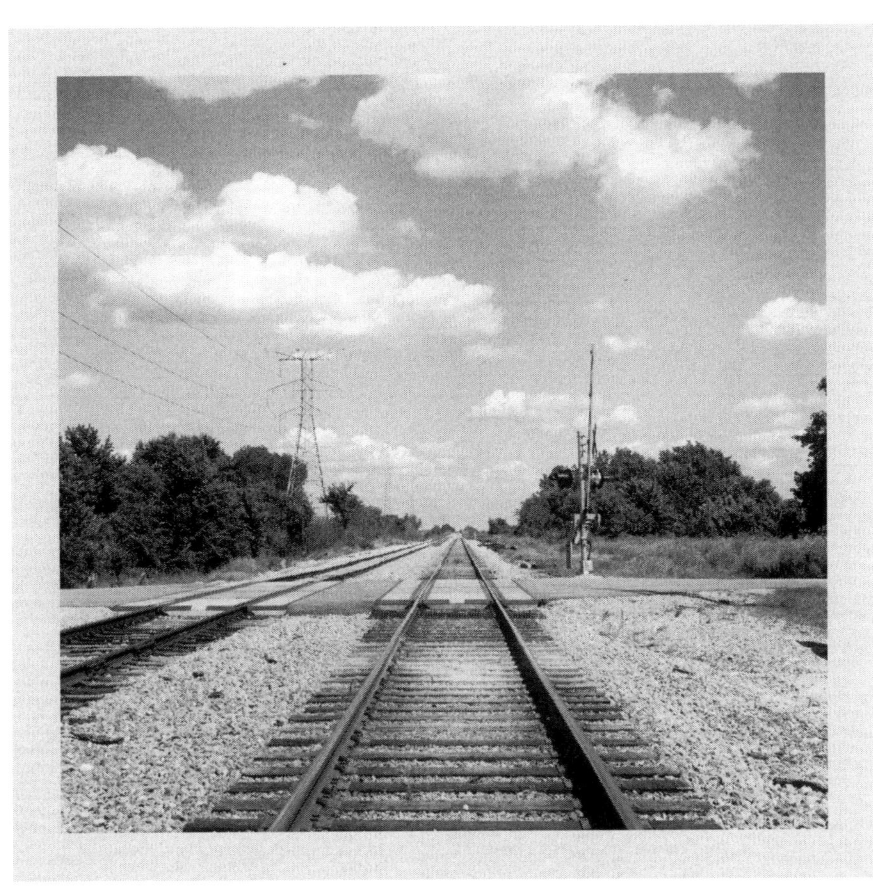

Field Notes

I.

The way is very simple. There is the present moment. An awareness of existence. A sense of the oneness of all things. Silence and wonder.

Being human, we seek order and meaning, and we try to keep busy. On the move, we feel alive. We hope to escape, at least defer, our death. Easy, then, never really to know life.

Of late, my practice is relatively simple. I travel daily the roads and byways in and around this prairie town. Often I photograph something that attracts my attention. At home, sitting at my desk, I write a few words for the day. A meditation. These few things make a life. Eventually, perhaps, not even the need for these.

Existence takes precedence. We begin with the wonder that anything at all exists. Ourselves included. Existence is a mystery that is entertained in our daily lives. We approach the mystery not by reasoned thought and argumentation, but by experience. Existentialists and mystics, our method is meditative, a meditation on everyday life.

There is the initial encounter. A crisis, perhaps. A stage of life entered. Suffering. Doubt. Joy. Illness. Time running out. Finally a sense of oneness, of love. All these I now experience. I am called.

I will watch closely, and I will experience the mystery. Make a visual record with my camera. Keep a pen and writing pad at hand. Remembering the goal is always beyond this material: compassion, love, and union with all that exists. At the end of my street, two trees—mulberry and elm—grow into one. Snow has fallen during the night.

In years of experience I have learned that the only reality we can know is in the present moment. The past no longer exists; the future is not yet. Our only hold on reality is the moment we are given. There is nothing to lose, nothing to gain. Things simply are as they are. Our words—and our actions—are grounded in the here and now.

The home for which I have searched all my life is very near. There is the realization that I am at home with all that exists. No need to search for home when it is with us all the time.

My desk is an altar. A second-hand desk, once belonging to the Archbishop of Saint Paul. A place where a few words are gathered daily. The light from the southern sky filters through the lace curtains.

These days of spring I travel the roads of DeKalb County. A windmill beside a creek once pumped water for livestock. I stop, gather my camera and tripod, and walk into the field. Redwing blackbirds flutter and call from top the aged wheel of the windmill. The sky is clear and without a cloud.

There are few duties in this life to be performed. I am nearing what the Hindu texts refer to as the fourth stage of life, when one becomes a renunciate, a sannyasi. This final stage is preceded by those of student, householder, and forest-dweller. In the final stage, we reflect on the mysteries of life and follow a practice of meditation. The fundamental character of the ascetic is to wander. Free and unbounded, we have time to explore the mystical realm within. Solitude is a welcome friend.

The only goal now is to realize the oneness of all, to know what we sometimes call God. The eternal, immortal state is thus attained. In the wandering, in the practicing of meditation, in the renunciation, the spirit is freed and the devotee attains union with the divine. This is the ancient Hindu message, the "royal secret" that Krishna promised to reveal: "I pervade the entire universe in my unmanifested form. All creatures find their existence in me. Those who worship me and meditate on me constantly, without any other thought, I will provide for all their needs." The ninth chapter of the Bhagavad Gita ends with these words: "Fill your mind with me; love me; serve me; worship me always. Seeking me in your heart, you will at last be united with me."

When we have experienced the union of subject and object, we say that we have known the sublime. But what do we call that which we are in union with? There are many names: the Supreme Being, Allah, Yahweh, Great Spirit, Nature, God, Tao. The names point to the same thing: union with that which is ultimately nameless and unknowable. Only thought—existentially conditioned—seeks to provide a name. We name to suit our purpose at hand.

Meister Eckhart observes that we are an intimate and inescapable part of the unknown, called God. We may separate ourselves in thought and action, from ourselves and from others, but the unity of oneness remains. When we realize, become conscious of, the oneness, we experience the sublime. I become what I see, and I see what I become. In order to see clouds in the sky, I become the clouds in the sky. I become, as Ralph Waldo Emerson phrased it in his essay on Nature, "a transparent eyeball," adding, "I am nothing, I see all." We may not grasp it, but we may become it.

In his travels to the deep north of Japan in the seventeenth century, Matsuo Bashō wrote haiku poetry fused with his experience along the way. He observed: "Your poetry issues of its own accord when you and the object have become one—when you have plunged deep enough into the object to see something like a glimmering there."

I travel along Base Line Road on a day in May. The sun shines overhead and the air is still. A cow stands in a small pond near the road. Camera fixed on the tripod, I stare into the ground glass. I am lost in infinite space. Who is the one seeing? Who is the photographer?

How may we be free to enjoy life? When asked the question, Mahatma Gandhi simply replied, "Renounce and enjoy." When we are not attached to the results of our action, we are free to enjoy life. Our reward is in the action itself. And the action is without purpose, intention, or choice. Things are as they are.

We are part of everything. My self is the Self of all creation. Understanding my true self, my native state, I am free to be happy, free to love: I cannot do otherwise. The Ashtavakra Gita states: "Be quiet. You are awareness itself." Or as Augustine says, "Love, then do as you like." Goodness will come from an awareness of our oneness with all things.

Trees on a sloping field. A fence line. A summer sky. Am I not one with these? Nothing to be done. There is happiness.

On a June morning, I drive up Annie Glidden Road to photograph the tree I have been watching all winter and spring. The field now is planted in corn. A landscape pleasant to the eye.

Edmund Burke, writing in the middle of the eighteenth century, suggested that the sublime is found in an emotional feeling brought about by the fear of pain and the sense of danger. In terror, we move outside of ourselves to something beyond. Sublimity resides in the coming together of an object and a perceiver. And there is nothing like the sense of terror to move one to another level of consciousness. Beauty is merely pleasant.

Suddenly, as I walk through the cornfield, a yellow crop-duster airplane, only a few feet from the ground, flies toward me. I see clearly the nozzles for the spraying of herbicides and pesticides. With the next turn of the airplane, I expect to be sprayed with the dangerous chemicals. But it is the field next to me that is to be sprayed. Still trembling, I photograph the landscape before me—as the airplane takes another swoop over the adjacent field.

The poet travels to the Alps. He spends the night at an inn at the edge of the valley. In the morning he walks into the mountains and gazes with awe at Mont Blanc. Soon after he writes his poem.

The sublime for Shelley is not in the merely beautiful and picturesque. But still there is the state of mind in which subject and object are fused. The imagination of the poet is fully identified with the empty, desolate, and silent landscape of the mountain. "All seems eternal now," he writes, midway in the poem. No need for a God to speak here.

All seems eternal when we see a landscape in the silence of the moment, when we allow ourselves to be struck with wonder. The eternal is known concretely when we are present, quiet, without thought of past or future, unbounded by time. Wittgenstein writes in his *Tractatus Logico-Philosophicus,* "If we take eternity to mean not infinite temporal duration, but timelessness, the eternal life belongs to those who live in the present."

I pass daily the crucifixion sculpture at the edge of Saint Mary's Cemetery. Evergreen trees surround the cross. My sense is one of awe and often terror. Beyond the theistic imagery, symbolizing resurrection and everlasting life, my eternity is in the silent, empty moment as I pass.

This morning the sounds of Gabriel Fauré's *Requiem* fill the house. Not the terrors of judgment found in other requiems for the dead; rather, Fauré's meditations are on the peace and glory of the eternal. The sun is about to shine through the cold rain clouds of this autumn morning. I have hopes of an afternoon on country roads with my camera. Perhaps a trip north to the family farm.

Josef Sudek photographed to the sounds of music. With his camera, walking the streets and bridges, the gardens, and cathedrals of Prague, he could be heard murmuring, "The music keeps playing." On Tuesday evenings, he and his artist friends would gather in his crowded studio and play on the gramophone the music of Bach, Mozart, Vivaldi, Dvořák, Stravinsky, and Janáček. On the California shores, Edward Weston was photographing to the sounds of a Bach Brandenburg concerto.

It is music that lures us beyond ourselves. An existence without music seems unbearable and impossible. Music transports us to an eternal realm, in the moment of hearing, where death has no place. Music and spiritual experience are inseparable.

How are we to make ourselves ready for the experience of the sublime? The meditative act of photographing is now my daily spiritual practice. And some reflection in the word. The disjunction between subject and object is overcome. Earth and sky are joined. I become one with nature.

The act of creating expands the spirit of the artist. The spiritual eye of the photographer beholds a landscape. Clouds following the rain form above the grain elevator. At the intersection of Highway 64 and Five Points Road—along the abandoned tracks of the Great Western Railway—a photograph is made.

At the end of his years, during the spring and summer of 1689, the poet Bashō walked the roads of northern Japan. He sold his house in Edo prior to his departure, not expecting to return from his wanderings. He took the open road in the spirit of Buddhist philosophy: life itself is a journey, a journey into eternity.

Along the way, Bashō was greeted by merchants, peasants, and monks. He rested and worshipped at Buddhist and Shinto shrines. He kept a journal of his five months of traveling, and he wrote haiku poems. The journey, for Bashō, and for all who travel with him, is life itself. In all that will perish, we seek a vision of eternity. Finally, in the Zen sense, we "return to original mind"— our connection to all that exists. Eternity is in codependent origination, in the interdependence of all things, arising and falling away. Our spiritual growth is in this realization.

Along Old State Road, I look for a place for rest and meditation. Another pilgrim on the road. A driveway leads to an old barn; a farmhouse is now gone. A No Trespass sign is nailed to a tree for anyone who would wish to stop. At the end of the driveway, I park and place the tripod on top of the car, and compose in silence. For a moment, this self is cast away in an eternity.

Keats is meditating on a Grecian urn. There is a juxtaposition of the static but immortal lifelessness of the artistic and pastoral scene on the urn and the vital experience of his own mortal life. Death is an escape from human decay, but Keats embraces life.

Paint peels from the weathering boards of the toolshed on the abandoned farm. Even that which is not human, but made from human life, decays and finally perishes. Without attachment, a Grecian urn or a farm shed can be appreciated without sorrow. The teacup, as a Zen Master informs us, will finally break. Nothing of this world, human or otherwise, is permanent.

The permanent—the formless and changeless—is beyond the existence of truth and beauty. Beyond imagination; beyond death. The cosmic vision of the Bhagavad Gita ultimately satisfies: "Changeless, you are what is and what is not, and beyond the duality of existence and nonexistence." Truth and beauty on the cosmic plane: "I am time, the destroyer of all."

After my classes of the day, I drive five miles west to the little town of Malta. A bright afternoon sun casts shadows along the main street that runs north and south. The white cement grain elevator rises beside the Chicago & North Western railroad tracks. Power lines, a parked car and truck, the Village Pizza. There is great joy as I stand in the street, camera resting on the tripod, and behold the moment. The world is loved, as am I—a part of everything.

For years, on my way to Rockford, I have passed the farm on Cherry Valley Road. I slow down to observe more closely the falling buildings. Two aging farmers move around the yard, going about their chores. Imagining the circumstances, the idle dreamer passes on the highway.

My daughter Laura once reminded me of Wordsworth's narrative poem "The Ruined Cottage." A wandering poet meets an aging peddler who tells "a common tale" of the woman who once lived in the cottage and longed for the return of her husband. After years of suffering and grief, Margaret has died and the cottage is in ruins. What are we—poets, peddlers, travelers—to make of a world in which such things happen?

Wordsworth's story-telling peddler finally realizes that human tragedy takes place within "the calm oblivious tendencies" of nature. Beyond our thoughts, beyond our idle dreaming, everything is taken back into the nature from where it came. The peddler walks along the road happily.

Lines go both ways—to and from. Railroads, electric power lines, telephones. Always leaving, arriving, and passing in between. Time marks the distance, and memory tries to make the connection.

William Stafford in his poem "The Farm on the Great Plains" attempts to make a connection at the end of the telephone line. "Hello, is Mother at home?" The vacancy of the home place—and the longing of the poet—is resolved in the realization that the caller is the called. No longer is there a line: "Then the line will be gone/because both ends will be home."

The tracks of the Illinois Central Railroad cross Cherry Valley Road to the east of Irene. I pause to photograph the lines on one of my aimless travels. There is neither coming nor going. No longing for what is not. I am that which is at the end of the line. For the moment, I am at home.

The photograph—the print from a negative, now on photographic paper—is a result of many experiences and decisions. For some time I have passed by the particular landscape. On this day—a Sunday afternoon—I have driven out to the abandoned farmstead, located on a new road that is to serve as a bypass around this growing town. I set up my camera and tripod, compose on the ground glass from various angles and distances, framing a possible exposure. I watch the sky for passing clouds; wait for starlings to settle on the power line; catch the gentle breeze on the tall grass. A negative is made in the release of the shutter cable. In the mixture of chemicals and light, and some time, a photograph appears.

The photograph before me has a presence about it, a feeling I perceive in the image beyond the artifice of paper and print. Walter Benjamin referred to this presence as an aura, an authenticity that is perceived by the viewer, diminished only in further reproduction out of the original context. Later, Roland Barthes would study a photograph of his mother, no longer living, and sense much more than the grain of the paper. In the reality of the photograph, the death of his mother is transcended. In gazing at the photograph, his mother exists again. More than nostalgia for what has passed, Barthes experiences something more authentic: the presence of his mother. The effect of the photograph is "not to restore what has been abolished (by time, by distance) but to attest that what I see has indeed existed." The experience is in the realm of the religious: "Photography has something to do with resurrection." Gazing into the viewfinder of the camera, I am part of the life, and the death, and the resurrection.

Several hundred years before the Christian era, Lao-tzu gave us the verses of the *Tao Te Ching*. The book that has come down to us, in its many translations, is a manual on the art of living. I return to the lines whenever there is need for simplicity, for letting things go without my interference. "When nothing is done, nothing is left undone."

On a Friday afternoon, I wander the country roads. I have been thinking about photographing a shed on the rise of a hill off Derby Line Road. The building, with a few surrounding trees, is all that remains from an abandoned farmstead. I had imagined a clear day with billowing clouds and a sharp afternoon light. Instead, on this humid day, vapor trails from jet airplanes cross the hazy sky. Without choice, the photographer takes what is given. Letting things go their own way.

Who am I? Who are you? We spend a lifetime making portraits of ourselves. We pause along the way, as artists, to make self-portraits of our true selves. We hope to see ourselves as we really are.

Thich Nhat Hanh reminds us that we have many names, and that we can recognize ourselves in each other. When any name is called, we answer yes. Please call me by my true names.

I look into the river that flows by my house. In a portrait taken from the bridge, I see my true self reflected in the flowing water. Within the shadow, among the grasses and the rocks, I see myself as the river flows.

Affirmed in the dialogue between Sri Krishna and Arjuna is the reality that pervades the impermanence of each passing moment. There is reality, an imperishable reality that dwells within us. Krishna adds: "Death is inevitable for the living; birth is inevitable for the dead. Since these are unavoidable, you should not sorrow. Every creature is unmanifested at first and then attains manifestation. When its end has come, it once again becomes unmanifested. What is to lament in this?"

At noon on Quarry Road, just west of Kirkland, I stop to gaze into the limestone quarry that is being worked into gravel. Below the topsoil that is host to prairie vegetation is the sediment of once a vast lake. And below that is still further manifestation of this earth. But there is that which is beyond all human digging and excavation. There is that which is indestructible, unchanging, imperishable. I take another glance, imagining the true reality.

Repeated in the Upanishads are the words *tat tvam asi:* "You are that." Ultimate reality is beyond the impermanence of our daily lives. In our unmanifested being, we are of that which is unmanifested. The Self of the cosmos is realized within each of us. I am that, the whole of reality. At home, as I stop on my travels and look into the depths of the quarry.

Edmund Burke would locate the sublime in landscapes signifying danger and eliciting terror in the beholder. Immanuel Kant later would suggest that it is the boundlessness of the sublime that moves us. John Milton, in the seventeenth century, imagined God's creation of the universe. Out of the abyss—out of chaos—an ordered world was created. We too behold the creation.

Any of these visions anticipate the nuclear world: the atom, the Bomb, and nuclear power. Is there not danger, perhaps the possibility of death, in the nuclear experimentation of our time? And may it not be that the splitting of the atom is the human attempt to know the source of the universe—to know God? It may be, as well, that we believe we cannot know ourselves (what is life?) until we can destroy that which is life. The sublime gone mad.

Standing at the edge of a pasture, along a fence line, I watch the steam bellow from the two cooling towers of Commonwealth

Edison's nuclear power plant at Byron. A sublime landscape in which I sense danger and, at the same time, the wonder of the energy of the universe. On heavenly ground, the line between the abyss and the creation is not wholly evident.

At home the sun streams through the hallway window upstairs. Lace curtains reflect on the wall. The oval mirror watches all. Laughing, perhaps, as I take another photograph.

The seeking is no longer as it once was. I practice the wonder, rather than striving for what is not. Being aware that the unknown, the inconceivable, is my original nature, there is little to be achieved. Things are as they are; I am as I am. Any effort of achievement would be further separation from everything else. In other words, I am unconditionally loved.

We are beyond choice. Alan Watts wrote sometime ago: "Getting out of your own way comes about when doing so ceases to be a matter of choice, because you see that there is nothing else for you to do." Neither doing, nor non-doing. Just being and letting be.

We are already one with reality. Already enlightened in the present moment. Further striving only removes us from reality. Gone are the long hours of sitting meditation. With camera and a few words, I simply watch.

This year's heron has left the cove that was its summer home. Cooling water laps against the dead trees and stumps protruding from the lake. Long ago the marsh and lowlands were flooded in the damming of a small creek to make the lake we now call Shabbona, for Chief Shabbona, the Potawatomi leader who once lived in the nearby grove. In DeKalb County, this is our wildness and our wet.

The Jesuit poet Gerard Manley Hopkins coined the word "inscape" to denote the unique intrinsic quality of a natural object as seen by the attentive observer. This quality is found even in dead things, in the "notable dead tree" he observed in a journal entry of the 1860s. The essence of the tree, of the waters, of all nature, is available to us if we will only see clearly. And in the seeing we become one with—in harmony with—what is seen.

Tractors and combines and corn pickers drive into the night. Waves of dust from rows of soybeans rise and pass over the light beams of the great machines that move through the fields. It is harvest time on the prairie.

The leaves of drying corn blow in the afternoon wind. I stop on the overpass outside of Shabbona, south of DeKalb, and make my way down the embankment. Rows of corn point north toward the horizon. Along the horizon are scattered farms and groves of trees. Light clouds float above. The truth and beauty of this world can be known in the meeting of earth and sky.

On the horizon, the mind's eye senses the sublime. Here is the expectation of what is beyond and cannot be seen. And more, at the end of the earth, at the edge that appears as horizon, is a joining with the sky, leading into a universe. On the brink of something greater than ourselves.

Union with the sacred is to be realized finally in the concrete experiences of everyday life. Saint Paul in his letter to the Corinthians says that he is nothing without love, pointing to God as the object of his love. But for most of us, whatever union we may know with mysteries beyond this world, love is found existentially with others on this earth. To love God is to love others, as ourselves, in our daily lives. The sacred and the secular are united, concretely, in love.

The mystical union is enacted each time one sees clearly enough to take a photograph. Alfred Stieglitz, in a question, speaks to Minor White of love and photography. Photography becomes integral to a life, becomes the heart of your life, and makes you more loving.

Yesterday afternoon, in the warm glow of the autumn sun, Solveig and I wandered over the paths of the restored prairie south of town. Dry stalks of Queen Anne's lace swayed in the light breeze. Cumulus clouds drifted above in the soft blue sky. A few remaining moths were flying and resting. We played in the fields.

This is the landscape to which I returned after years of traveling in other places. It is a landscape of transcendent quality, having to do with the line of the horizon, the way the sky meets the land, the drift of the clouds over the fields and towns, the way the sun reflects against the weathered barn.

Photographing the landscape, I have discovered the importance of watching all things as they rise and pass away, of seeing things as they really are. Experiencing the landscape in silence, with bare attention, I become aware of the absolute nothingness of the world, of the reality beyond words. Everything of which I am part is immeasurable and mysterious.

The road is the way to eternity. The journey is inward to an unknown universe, and home is where I have never been before. Here, on this road, as I travel, I am at home.

The naturalist John Muir grew up on a farm near Portage, Wisconsin. As a child, he had emigrated from Scotland with his parents. Life on the farm was harsh, and John eventually went to the state university, and worked on his mechanical inventions. He walked from the Midwest to the Gulf of Mexico, keeping a journal along the way. In 1868, he traveled to Yosemite Valley in California. National forests and parks were preserved from commercial development under his inspiration. He camped in the wilderness.

John Muir wrote beautifully of the natural world. "We all dwell in a house of one room," he told us. We walk this earth under the arch of the sky. To conserve this earth and this firmament above is to protect and secure our own lives. We are intimate parts of the cosmos, completely interdependent. We all are under one roof.

The high power lines extend from the Mississippi River to Chicago, cutting through the rich fields of Illinois. Energy of the universe is harnessed in our time. Over the cornfields and through our bodies, electromagnetic forces are being made known to us. Suburbs and industries stretch west from Chicago. New housing developments are filling the fields.

And yet, within this landscape, we are in fact sailing through space. John Muir reminds us that nature prevails. When this landscape—of farms, industries, power lines, and houses—is gone, the earth and its firmament will remain. We, you and I, leave no traces. May we live today in the landscapes of our creation with such ecological awareness. Our true nature, we know: "sailing the celestial spaces without leaving any track."

A late autumn morning after a night of frost. The few remaining leaves on the trees shake against the wind. The birds have gone. A vacant, abandoned house on Irene Road stands in ruins from life of another time.

Ruins appeal to the romantic imagination. Here is a sense sublime, an awareness of the union of past and present in the active forces of nature. Our human works of art and habitation are finally consumed in a new unity—the ruin. "Let it decay," Georg Simmel declared in an essay written nearly a hundred years ago. Simmel added: "It is the fascination of the ruin that here the work of man appears to us entirely as a product of nature. The same forces which give a mountain its shape through weathering, erosion, faulting, and the growth of vegetation, here do their work on old walls." From the earth we come and to the earth we return.

A peace surrounds the house in ruins on Irene Road this autumn day. The life that once dwelled here—in all its daily pursuit—is present in this moment. Nature's wisdom prevails. In the ruin we know the eternal.

I observe carefully the decaying log found on my walk today through the woods on the Ellwood grounds. A time to renew the lesson of ecology—of the Dharma: Life and death are interdependent. One does not exist without the other. Where is the line between the living fungus and the rotting wood that nourishes it? The log is host. The world is held together by death and decay.

Death is but a human conception, made out of fear. Only the conditioned mind would call the leaf "dead" falling from the tree today. The leaf has spent the summer filling the tree with life. The energy of the leaf is in the growth of the tree. The leaf that falls is but an artifact; life is elsewhere. No death on this day.

A trip south of town to the grove in what is now called the Chief Shabbona Forest Preserve. Snow covers the trunks and branches of fallen oaks. Once the chief of the Potawatomis made a home here. Later, after the grove had been seized in land dealings, he would be seen on his black and white pony, an aged rider moving along the rivers and across the prairies of northern Illinois, wife and grandchildren in the wagon. He painted his face black after advising Black Hawk to make the peace: Armies of whites are without number, like sands of the sea. Ruin will follow all who go to war. Rolled up in a blanket, Chief Shabbona slept out the cold nights.

Great fallen trees in the cover of snow this gentle day. Fields of corn, yet with grazing deer, surround the grove. I wait, and watch, as the night approaches.

Snow falls easily this December, beginning in the night and continuing into the day. The last corn from the field is being shelled and hauled to the large metal bins. Steam bellows from the gas-powered driers, as the corn is relieved of its moisture. Along the railroad tracks and in the yards of farms, the steaming grain bins signal the end of another harvest.

Last week a friend who is an Anglican rector in a parish near Bristol visited me. He told me the story about the bishop, found by a parishioner, browsing through a book of erotic photographs in a London bookstore. Given a disapproving eye, the bishop quoted scripture: "To the pure all things are pure, but to the corrupt and unbelieving nothing is pure." The world—in all its variety—is made known to us by the minds we have created in a lifetime.

I park my car deep in the snow at the edge of the highway. I walk ankle deep to the top of the snow-covered cornfield, and photograph the steaming corn bins in the distance, along the tracks of the Chicago & North Western. The warm light of a late afternoon is on my back as the sun fast approaches the far horizon. Long shadows are cast on the field.

Fresh snow on the ground and a fog over the fields. On the day of Creation, according to Genesis, "a mist rose up from the land and moistened the whole face of the earth." Barren ground was turned into fertile fields. A mist rising up from the land will last all this day.

I drive slowly the road that leads east out of town. Beside the road, on the fresh earth of the field, a farmer has made stacks of shredded cornstalks. Winter bedding for the cattle. All day I will stay with the fog. Near the end of the day I will stand before the crumbling foundation of a barn, knee-deep in snow, among the decaying weeds and scrubs, pine tree rising in the fog.

The early nineteenth-century paintings of Caspar David Friedrich play in the mind's eye as I wander the roads and byways of northern Illinois this winter. Friedrich's range of subjects was limited: ruins, churches, graveyards, times of day, sea and mountains, trees, and the light of dawn and dusk, fog and mist. And within these subjects, the painter was a contemplative, one with nature, gazing outward toward an infinite distance. On the edge of the natural world, in the realm of the timeless, the luminous nothingness, the void. We "merge," as the old Zen master Yuanwuy said, "with the boundless and become wholly empty and still." Photographing, on this fog-filled, misty, snowy day, life is just this.

On Annie Glidden Road, I stop and photograph the homesteader's cemetery, known locally as the Vandeburg Cemetery. One-half acre of falling and fading tombstones, burials from the 1850s. A single evergreen tree stands in the mist—an ancient symbol of the everlasting life. Again, nature prevails; and I know once more, in solitude, my true being.

The first full snow of winter. Yes, James Joyce would write, snow is general all over the county. It fell on the prairie south of town, and on the shallow waterways along the plowed fields. It fell, too, upon the country churchyards and on the headstones and on the branches of the evergreen. This is the day of epiphany, as well.

A faintly falling snow as I park at the entrance of Saint Mary's Cemetery on County Line Road and walk among the gravestones. The closing lines of Joyce's story "The Dead" are in my thoughts. "Better pass boldly into that other world, in the full glory of some passion, than fade and wither dismally with age." My passions are simple, but they are passions, and they are at the center of my life: the wonder of existence each day, writing and photographing, and the love of those held dearly. Nothing is separate; all is holy. I listen to the snow falling through the universe, upon all the living and the dead.

As old as the Vedic hymns is the habit of the human spirit to pose a duality. Nearly all cults and religions depend upon a separation between this life and some other world beyond everyday existence. Almost as if we humans need to be strangers to the world in order to feel deeply or to entertain the mystery of life. As if we need to imagine that we belong to some other place. That the present is not enough. Out of such needs and thoughts gods are created.

But is there not another way? The way beyond dualism, the way of oneness. There is no transcendence apart from this life. This life itself is the measure and source of all value. The sublime is in the wonder of daily life, rather than in the reaching for something of another world. No myth-making, no God-making, but affirmation of this life.

And where does this world come from? What is the source of our being? Let us call it the void. Out of the void we have come, out of non-being, and to the void we return. Birth is but a manifestation of non-being. Death is a return to our non-being, to the void. Rilke, in *The Sonnets to Orpheus,* instructs us to be in this life—"and yet know the great void where all things begin." We are here, completely and sublimely, when we merely let go to the moment. The way is very simple.

On the other side of town, there is a stand of pine trees growing on the flood plain beside the Kishwaukee River. I walk into the woods on this cold and snowy day. A silence, a void, the source of my being. Just letting go.

Still the blueness of morning light. I have returned to the snowy fields along Five Points Road. A telephone line. Frost-covered trees lining an unnamed gravel road. Last fall's dried weeds sprouting from snow banks. Farm animals standing in the cold, backs to the warming eastern sky. A few crows fly over a distant woods.

Søren Kierkegaard confides to his journal, in the winter of 1846, that once he aspired to become a minister in a rural parish and live amid quiet scenery. The bishop, in fact, had such hopes for him, that he might become somebody important. But there is the rub, confides Kierkegaard, "I aspire to be as little as possible," and "that is precisely the core of my melancholy." Kierkegaard is content to be, as he says, "half-mad," something out of the ordinary. This is quite possibly to "remain my essential form of existence," he observes, "and I shall never attain the pleasant becalmed existence of being something very small."

The melancholy, I know. And it does have to do with choosing a path and living its truth. And I know the innermost existence of Kierkegaard's life: "Only when I write do I feel well. Then I forget all of life's vexations, all its sufferings, and I am wrapped in thought and am happy. If I stop for a few days, right away I become ill, overwhelmed and troubled; my head feels heavy and burdened." The same can be said of the photograph taken on days of need, and of the few meditative words offered in the stillness of home.

I pass a fence line that is interspersed every few yards with thickets of trees and shrubs. Stopping, and singling out one for examination, I find that the thicket is a summer's branching from the stump of a sawed-off tree.

Caspar David Friedrich, in the winter of 1828, painted such a thicket on a heath he knew well outside of Dresden. His thicket was a cluster of bare alders. The painting he made was of his experience of standing before the thicket. Just as my photograph of the thicket of sprouting silver maple branches is an expression of my experience on this winter's day. I pause in my travels to behold a certain thicket, along a fence line, on a ground of snow.

At home, I hold a twig snapped from the thicket. The twig guide to trees and shrubs clearly identifies the thicket: *Acer saccharinum,* Silver Maple. Twig red, rank with odor when crushed; bud bright red. The buds are swelling, preparing in the middle of winter for the new and tender leaves of spring. Already, signs of renewal, rebirth, and resurrection.

In the book *Looking at Photographs,* John Szarkowski discusses Harry Callahan's photograph "Eleanor, Port Huron." A photograph taken in 1954 of Callahan's wife among tender shots of sumac. Like so many of Callahan's photographs, it is a composition made in the course of everyday life—of materials close at hand. A photograph that is in relation to one's life. But more than this, Szarkowski writes: "The point is that for

Harry Callahan photography has been a way of living—his way of meeting and making peace with the day."

A bright winter afternoon. It is Sunday and the snow is still fresh. Solveig and I drive a few miles north to the bridge where the Kishwaukee River flows under Annie Glidden Road. This day of worship.

Sometimes you will see a horse. Perhaps several, backs to the wind on the side of a snow-covered hill. Today a light, dappled horse stands near the road.

In childhood, a deep pond filled a kettle in the moraine near the farm. Protruding from the water was the head of a wooden horse. We anticipated the wonder each time we approached the pond on the way to town. Only later would I learn the Greek myth of Pegasus, the winged horse that left the earth and entered the heavens.

Bellerophon, the grandson of Sisyphus, rode the winged horse in pursuit of the monster Chimera. The fire-breathing monster is slain, and Pegasus is never mounted again by any mortal being. The fate of Bellerophon varies by the telling. Some say that fame went to his head, that he grew vain from the thought that he was as great as the gods that he lost his soul and wandered until he died. As for Pegasus, Jupiter set the divine horse among the stars. The constellation in the sky is a reminder of our immortality, at least a symbol of our creative imagination.

As I return to the road, the same mind that recalls Pegasus remembers the passage from Revelation: "And I looked, and behold a pale horse; and its rider was Death." In the rearview mirror, I see the horse on the other side of the fence carefully watching me.

There is something—grand, otherworldly—about oaks in the winter landscape. You see the trees standing on a savanna in the middle of a prairie, or on a glacial ridge to the north. Oaks make the vast wooded park on the edge of town. On this day in January, the trunks and limbs of barren oaks extend into the cold sky. One imagines a ruined cloister in a grove of oaks. A seeker in the snow, I hear a brief requiem to the dead.

Looking for my old friend who died ten years ago. Like Wang Wei, poet of the T'ang dynasty, I search for the meaning of his death. A friend of the woods, an anthropologist of the world, my friend Tony now is nowhere to be found. He walked into the oak woods on a winter's day. We never saw him again. Some of his work remains, a reputation. Yet, the reality of this death, the empty woods.

We both, descendants of the ancient Celts, had imagined those who lived in the oak forest. Druids, priests and teachers, knew the oaks, worshipped the oaks. Found immortality in the trees. We still do.

Thoughts of Tennyson's long poem *In Memoriam.* The poem was composed over the years, a series of elegies for his friend of many years, Arthur Henry Hallam. Another search for the meaning of death. Tennyson finds his consolation in "some diffusive power," in that which we continue to call God. Found in star and flower, in our loving, on the rolling air, in the running waters, in the rising sun.

And now, before me, a picket fence rises out of a bank of snow beside the road. Pointing to that "one far-off divine event." Tennyson's last line suffices: "To which the whole creation moves."

Most sublime is Claude Debussy's opera *Pelléas et Mélisande*. On a cold night we rode the train to Chicago and walked the few blocks against the winds of Lake Michigan to the Lyric Opera House. The libretto, adapted from a play by the symbolist poet Maurice Maeterlinck, is chanted to a continuous flow of the musical score.

A Nordic setting, in a mythical kingdom called Allemonde, "all the world." The lives, loves, and destiny of four generations are being played out in the dark days and cold nights beside the stormy sea. The principals consist of Arkel the king; Golaud, his grandson; Pelléas, the half brother of Golaud; Geneviève, the daughter of Arkel and mother of Golaud and Pelléas; and Mélisande the loved one, the soprano. They often speak of the cold, the darkness, and of the great unknown.

Some weeks later I read the stories and poems of Edgar Allan Poe. Poe's writings had influenced the European symbolists, including Maeterlinck and Debussy. The mystery of a place, the uncertainty of human life, and always the melancholy. I read again the last lines of "Annabel Lee," Poe's elegy to loves past. The same day I walk to the graveyard behind the Congregational church, only a few blocks from my house, camera in hand. To make my own poem.

On board ship, returning to France after several weeks in New York and Canada, in the spring of 1946, Albert Camus looks into the sea and up into the night sky. All the ambivalence in the world: "That's the way the sea is," Camus exclaims, "and that's why I love it! A call to life and an invitation to death." Continuing in his journal, Camus writes, "Yes, I've loved the sea very much — this calm immensity — these wakes folded under wakes — liquid routes. For the first time a horizon that measures up to the breath of a man, a space as large as his audacity."

Just south of town, on the corner of Alva and Waterman roads, a large, long-ago abandoned house stands among ice-covered thickets and trees. A train rolls along the tracks that pass the empty grain elevator. Two white dogs approach on the gravel road and stop to sniff my camera gear. The temperature will not rise above five degrees Fahrenheit today. On this expanse of prairie, my existence finds its measure. Sweetness this day where ice crystals form in the sun. A cold silence.

On a voyage in the night, Camus desires to be made "the equal of these seas of forgetfulness, these unlimited silences that are like the enchantment of death." South of town, standing before an ice palace, I too for the moment am free of everything.

The winding south branch of the Kishwaukee River crosses the road south of town and meanders across the vast expanse of cultivated prairie. Farm buildings dot the horizon on this winter day.

Paul Bowles writes at the beginning of his journal, published as *Days*, that his account demonstrates "the way in which the hours of a day can as satisfactorily be filled with trivia as with important events." Which is also to say that the daily accounting allows us to give attention to the ultimate mystery, the ordinary living of each day. Everything is worthy of note when we cease to look for the important events.

Wherever we are, we are in a specific and unique place. And as Bowles observes in a biographical reflection: "My life consists of the places where I have lived and the work I have accomplished in those places." My life and work also can be charted by the places I have lived; I am a sum of where I have been. But right now, in the only reality there is, I am on a prairie south of town, standing before a creek flowing through a field in winter..

The month of February is nearing an end, the groundhog has returned to its burrow on the hill beside the river, and I am about to leave for two weeks of lecturing in the Netherlands. This morning I returned to the elm tree at the end of our street. The elm a year ago stood entwined with the mulberry tree. Today, the mulberry is being removed by chain saws. Mulberry and sections of the elm are scattered on the ground where once two trees grew into one.

The line from Ecclesiastes comes to mind these days, especially when an accomplishment is sensed: "This too is futility and a chasing of the wind." The author of Ecclesiastes, writing three hundred years before Christ, examines the accomplishments of life—material riches, knowledge and wisdom, the fruits of labor—and finds them all unable to give meaning to life. Life, the author concludes, is uncertain, hidden of meaning, and the ways of God are incomprehensible. The only conclusion to this human condition is to accept gratefully the pleasures of everyday life. Life is a mystery, not to be solved, but to be enjoyed and appreciated.

If there has been a path to my living over the last few years, it is near the one followed by the author of Ecclesiastes. In Zen terms, all endeavors are empty and devoid of substance. The meaning of life—all the meaning we can know—is in the living of it. Even in our suffering. The profit of work is in the doing of it; we are not, according to Hindu scripture, to be attached to any other results. And the only mastery we have over birth and death is in the realization of our true nature, of our true self. This is the unitive state that we experience as human beings. Wondrous is our existence, the living of it now.

All the days in Amsterdam we read from Albert Camus's novel *The Fall*. It's the story of a modern man, Jean-Baptiste Clamence, an expatriate Frenchman, a former lawyer now living in Amsterdam. Clamence has spent a lifetime in noble causes and has been a pursuer of the libertine life. And as a judge of all around him, he is serving time as a "judge-penitent." His office, not far from Central Station, is the bar, the café, known as Mexico City.

Amsterdam is a city of concentric canals that resemble to Clamence the circles of hell. People come from all corners of the earth, listen to the foghorns, make out the silhouettes of boats in the fog, and return in the rain to houses wedged into little spaces. In Amsterdam, we had a wonderful time.

But what the book is about, and what we experienced one turn after another, was the heavy hold of morality, of a morality that is necessarily realized in daily judgments by the thousands. No need to wait for the Last Judgment for we are judged, and we judge, every day of our lives. We are slaves to order, to judgment, to violence and punishment. In our philosophy and in our religion, and in our daily lives, we are never innocent; we are always guilty. Where is the love is such a world?

The realization once again: the only order, the only morality that we need is in the living of the moment, close to reality. Beyond the ego-self. A compassionate oneness with all things, human and otherwise. Back home in Illinois, a few signs of spring. At the edge of town, the winter's accumulation of wrecked automobiles is piled high in the steel-fenced yard.

In Georges Bernanos's novel *The Diary of a Country Priest,* when the country priest is dying, a friend at his bedside has sent for the parish priest to come and offer the final consolations of the church. But the country priest utters his final words: "Does it matter? Grace is everywhere..."

I am waiting for the year's renewal. Everywhere the signs seem to be delayed. Someday I will be moved to make a photograph, although I know that any shot will do. The signs are simply in the seeing. Everywhere, the eternal. All is grace. Yet, I wait.

But wait for what? The kingdom has already arrived. As reported in the Gospel of Thomas, the disciples ask Jesus, "When will the kingdom come?" And he answers, "What you are waiting for has already come, but you don't recognize it." There is nothing further to be grasped, nothing to be rejected; grace is everywhere. Blessed are the pure in heart, for they will see, and they will be the makers of peace.

Where we started—confronting our existence and our mortality. Affirming the oneness. Our human condition of having to find meaning in the course of everyday life. No universal meaning otherwise being evident. This is where we know grace.

Waiting for execution, in Camus's *The Stranger,* Meursault speaks of the wonder of his existence: "In that night alive with signs and stars, I opened myself to the gentle indifference of the world." Could there be more wonder than this?

Existence is our essence. In all of our humanity, we are what we think and what we do, and what we see each day. We become one, now, in this moment. The sublime is everywhere. All is eternal.

II.

A train speeds through the night and enters another prairie town. The whistle blows, a scream into the dark night. Townspeople in their beds turn with a shudder. Dreams already underway take another direction. With luck, on a good night, sleep returns. There is hope for another day.

In the morning—this morning of a rising sun in a clear sky—one person in town gets out of bed and goes to the room that is his study. He opens the closet and removes the camera. Film is placed into the magazine, and a yellow filter is fitted over the lens. Give the morning some more time. Then walk downtown to begin the day's work. Although he does not yet know it, there will come a time when he will question this life of being a spectator, of being a detached observer in the quest for knowledge.

I am that person. The one who now lives here after living in many other places. A life of wandering, yes. But that is not the point of this telling. What we have for the time being is this place, a prairie town in the northern hemisphere of the planet Earth, located on the spiral arm of a galaxy called the Milky Way, at the end of an era known as the twentieth century. All this is a part of something called the universe. I will tell you more.

Throughout these days, these days of our unease, we make our way downtown. The ultimate questions loom over us. Being and non-being, fullness and emptiness, God and the great abyss.

The age—our contemporary existence—might be characterized as the age of Time Being. We are between ages, yet we have a foot in both: the modernism of the past century and the post-modernism of the future. For the present, we have only what is possible, the time being. And, as W. H. Auden has told us, "The Time Being is, in a sense, the most trying Time of all." In the present, we live daily to redeem ourselves from insignificance. Astride the abyss, we are alive.

The look of this place, this town within which I wander, reflects our time. A landscape that is ambiguous, impermanent, and of mixed and multiple sensibilities. As I walk the streets, make my stops, as I wait for the trains to pass through town, I experience the world as film noir. An Edward Hopper landscape of isolated buildings, abandoned storefronts, a highway along the main street, filling stations old and new, the interiors of restaurants and coffee shops, a melancholy in the air, shadows and light.

A vision has been granted unto us. In the ordinary is the strange and the magnificent. This is our time to be lived in wonder and in compassion. Nighthawks by both day and night, we make our investigations. Ethnographers of everyday life at the close of a century, we sense if not a new beginning, at least a world of many possibilities.

And these possibilities come in a remove from the idolatries that continue to surround us. With the novelist Milan Kundera, I hope for "the wisdom of uncertainty," and for the courage to entertain the ambiguity of the human condition. Most religions and ideologies are founded on a desire for a clear distinction between good and evil, on the need to judge and to punish. Might I, as I walk these streets, witness the essential relativity of things human? Might I look squarely at the absence of a Supreme Judge? I might then know what it is to be truly human, to be connected compassionately to one another, and to be an integral part of the world.

Henry David Thoreau—in another time of cultural crisis—decided to live where he could practice the daily discipline "of looking always at what is to be seen." From his cabin on Walden Pond, he lived deliberately and observed closely the wonders of everyday life. Near the beginning of his accounting, in the book *Walden,* he noted the sounds he heard as he sat in the doorway of his cabin. There were the calls of the birds, the baying of dogs, the distant lowing of cows, the rumbling of wagons over bridges, the ringing of bells in the town, and the chanting of whippoorwills and the wailing of owls in the night. But most of his chapter on sounds is devoted to the trains as they pass on the rails at the edge of the pond a hundred rods south of his cabin. Once again, I feel affinity to Thoreau as yet another train passes through this town, only four blocks from my house. The train whistle unites us over the centuries. We hear much as the train passes.

A century's economy and industry, the ways of communication, the sense of time and discipline are conveyed in the whistle of the train. While Thoreau imagined the steaming locomotive as an iron horse, as a great steed snorting smoke from his nostrils and shaking the earth at his feet, I imagine something of another age. A great machine, diesel fueled, with a sound more piercing. And no passengers here on these trains, as compared to Thoreau's trains carrying travelers to Boston and returning them to the country west of Concord. My train carries freight only, speeding east to Chicago, and transporting goods back to the West: corn, coal, oil, refrigerated meats, cars and trucks, cement and steel building materials, and the long lines of piggy-backed boxes on flatbed cars.

The whistle of the train penetrates Walden woods, "sounding like the scream of a hawk sailing over some farmer's yards." Here in DeKalb, repeated blasts of the horn shoot into the bedrooms of our homes. Awakened, across a century and a half, we all are made to feel that we are citizens of the world. With Thoreau, my life has "become my amusement" and never ceases to be novel. No need to look elsewhere for the meaning of existence at the end of this twentieth century. It is here as another train passes through town.

The snows came and covered the ground during the holidays. A cold morning, this morning, and the wind is blowing with a chill of thirty below. The temperature will not rise above zero today.

Change, all is change, nothing remains the same. Not long ago, we went to the basement to get relief from the sweltering heat of the afternoon. At night we slept there for relief from the noise of the speeding trains loaded with the summer harvest. This morning, bundled in wool, I make a few notes while listening to Beethoven's last symphony, number nine in D minor. I listen, as well, to the songs of Lou Reed and John Cale in memory of Andy Warhol. With a little more sun, later in the morning, I will drive to the lumberyard. On my way, I hope to photograph the tracks along the abandoned passenger station.

Perhaps it is because of the impermanence of all things that we value life so dearly. And in accepting impermanence, we lessen the suffering that comes in holding on to that which cannot be saved. All things decay and change to something else, this body and self included. I live daily in this town with a faith in what cannot be fully known.

The epistemology of our time is in the attention we give to the world of appearance. In the Western world, we have dwelt in Plato's cave, between the fire and the wall, watching the shadows dance. But always the yearning for a clearer vision of the thing itself. To be enlightened in some manner. Through our imaginations and our daily observations, we give a semblance of order to what we experience. We make order out of chaos.

Everything is simply as it is. All is perfect: the earth turns, the seasons come and go, the tides rise and fall. We may at times, with some enlightenment, sense the emptiness (the fullness and the oneness) of the ultimate and the absolute. Being human—in body, mind, and heart—we must necessarily give our attention to the relative problems of our existence. The moral questions, however relative they may be, are the questions by which we live daily. Yet we live in two worlds, the absolute and the relative. Such is the problem of being human.

This day on my way home from the tracks I invoke the Sanskrit word *tathata.* An incantation to the ultimate and the absolute. The "suchness" of reality: everything is as it is, beyond the knowing mind. Reality-in-itself. In the darkening afternoon, I entertain beyond human experience the notion that nothing is born and nothing is dying. Birth and death exist only on the relative plane.

At home I read the words of Thich Nhat Hanh on the waves in the water. "Observing the ocean, we see that the waves are always there being born and being destroyed. A wave seems to have a beginning and an end. But waves are also water. If a wave is capable of seeing itself as water, it transcends all beginnings and all endings. As far as the waves are concerned, there may be birth and death, but as far as the water is concerned, no birth and no death can be found anywhere. Only if the wave realizes that it is water can it be emancipated from birth and death. When you look into the nature of interbeing, when you know that you are that nature of interbeing, you will be free."

What appears to be film noir—small town noir—in my daily human existence is simply emptiness, or *suchness,* in the realm of the absolute. I may die to the day (I *will* die to the day), but in a larger perspective there will be no death. I know this in moments of awareness, but still there will be the chill in my spine when the train from the west passes through town tonight and sounds its lonely whistle.

I hope to photograph the moving train as it passes through town. My attempts up to now have come to naught. Three or four freight trains speed through DeKalb every hour, twenty-four hours a day. But when I wait with the camera on the tripod, no trains appear. I am beginning to sense what it was like for Peter Matthiessen climbing the Himalayas and hoping to sight the snow leopard. Finally, as in all journeys, it is the search itself that is important.

At home, at the place I now call home, the whistle can be heard again. A nineteenth-century technology—the train and the whistle. A blasting of the whistle once removed cattle from the right-of-way granted the railroads. Today, a century and a half later, the whistle ceases to serve public safety. Accidents at the crossings and suicides along the tracks are recorded each year in town. I have written to the local newspapers protesting the noise of the train and the ineffectiveness of the whistle. I may be learning to live with trains, as I watch and wait and listen.

Earlier this year, a colleague in the history department observed how our minds reside in disciplines with regional, national, international, and sometimes cosmic directions. Yet, we live daily as citizens, as responsible human beings, here in town. Our bodies and emotions are attached to this place, but only portions of our minds dwell here. Much of the time we are not "here" at all. We make our accommodations, our adjustments; for me, the events of the here and now—in this Midwest town—are the substance of my intellectual work. The local and global become one and the same. Not just this train in this town, but *the* train—as fact and metaphor—in this turn-of-the-century existence.

Is it not, then, essentially a question of being at home? Our human impulse is to feel at home, to be at one with a place, a place that finally may be the whole of the universe. And it is with some sense of home, of belonging to a place, that we humans have, as Stanley Cavell has noted, "the promise and power of leaving it." With home, we have the possibility of leaving home, of distancing ourselves from the familiar, of wandering into a larger world. Thoreau, in building a cabin in the woods near Concord, was free to travel a whole world. Each day we leave home. As a wanderer, in thought and spirit as well as in space, I leave town each day.

We are firmly within a philosophical tradition, whether of the East or the West. Friedrich Nietzsche, as a European, wrote: "If you would like to see our European morality for once as it looks from a distance, and if one would like to measure it against other moralities, past and future, then one has to proceed as a wanderer who wants to know how high the towers in a town are: he *leaves* the town." And whether the objective is to compare or simply to live, the wanderer leaves home and enters the marketplace—with helping hands. Leaving home, for whatever duration, is an act of discovery, an act of being human in relation to all others.

I know that I will never be fully at home in this town or in this world. We all are ultimately of some other place; we are born to this world, and we leave it. In the meantime, we search for home and, simultaneously, we long to distance ourselves from it. Such is our human condition.

Yesterday, after a snowfall during the night, I set up my camera at Seventh Street to photograph the tracks. Without expectation, without thought or hope, what do you suppose happened? A train from the west roared toward me, and I quickly pushed the shutter release. The camera on the tripod was overturned by the force of the passing train. Recovering the camera in the snow, I may have captured on film the image of the train. Snow blew in the wind as the train sped out of town toward Chicago.

For some time, I have been reading Robert Burton's *The Anatomy of Melancholy,* that seventeenth-century book which continued to be revised until the author's death in 1640. The writing—and the immense reading upon which the writing is based—was Burton's life. Reading and writing were for Burton life itself.

I read *The Anatomy of Melancholy* for the same reasons today that Burton wrote the book three and half centuries ago. To keep busy and to occupy this gift of the human mind. The paradox of such labor, however: in distracting myself from the ultimate meaning of existence, I raise questions that lead me only further into the abyss.

Burton's book may be known best as a vast dissertation on the psychological state known as melancholy. It is certainly that, a book filled with the immense learning of the past, but it is also (if not primarily) a document of one person attempting to master the proliferation of learning available in published form. The invention of the printing press a century and a half before Burton's time made scholarship readily accessible, and made reading an occupation in itself. Melancholy, sometimes a morbid sadness, was a mental state many claimed to suffer in Burton's century.

The melancholy that concerned and afflicted Burton is the mental and psychological condition that comes with the search for knowledge. The more Burton read about melancholy, the more he tried to know the meaning of melancholy, the more he experienced melancholy. And is this not our condition today as intellectuals? The more we seek to know, the more we devise methods of investigation, the more depressed in mind and spirit we become.

Yet we continue to seek the holy grail of knowledge. I enter the local bookstore to place an order for a book that I have seen reviewed or cited in something I have read. Perhaps one more book will provide me with the answer (the answer to what?), or one more reading will set me on the right course. I enter the bookstore as if entering a temple, a sanctuary, a sacred place. There is ever the hope of salvation, of finding myself in the word. My bookcases at home are filled with books yet to be read. This winter I have built two more bookcases to hold the overflow.

More snow fell during the night. I will stay indoors and read. I will not worry, or speculate, about the missing mass in the universe that is reported in the morning newspaper. The earthquake on the other side of the planet is enough for one day. The distant whistle of the train brings me to attention. Loneliness is only a thought.

The abiding passion for Robert Burton—lasting a lifetime—was melancholy. Mine has been the search for reality. What is real, and how can reality be known? How Platonic the questions are, in thought and belief. An order is assumed, an order of "forms" (or "ideas") that transcends observation and experience, a higher realm, preexistent and eternal. We assume that the human mind, in all its reason, can apprehend a world beyond things physical.

Such is the Western belief system: There is a reality beyond our everyday experience, and this reality can be known by the human mind. There is more to existence than appearance; there is an essence beyond our own sense experience. A Western religion, the belief in something that is beyond this world, an eternal unknown, sometimes called God. We are mystics, then, in our spiritual and intellectual lives. We hope to see beyond the shadows of the cave.

Yet this mind of ours cannot know of the existence of anything beyond experience. The mind is limited by its own evolutionary capacity. This grand piano of a mind that provides the space for the music (our thoughts) to be played. We humans cannot step outside of our existence; we cannot know if there is anything outside of the grand piano. And we do not know if our existence is other than a dream.

It is not for us to know what cannot be known. To seek such knowledge is beyond our capacity as human beings. The simple teaching of Buddhism wisely informs us: "Only don't know." We have the mind to ask questions of reality, existential and ultimate, but we do not have the capacity to answer the questions. Such is our human condition, as Albert Camus said, a condition of the absurd. Humility, mixed with wonder, makes more sense than the continuous pursuit of trying to know what cannot be known.

We stand before the mystery of existence. Our humanity is in the recognition of our common inability to know for certain. Our fate, and our saving grace, is to be compassionate human beings. Whatever we attempt to know is known in love. Not in manipulation and control, not in the advancement of a separate self, but in the care for one another. This is reality enough.

In the wisdom of the East, the other word for reality is *enlightenment*. A realm of neither knowing nor not knowing.

Neither existence nor nonexistence. Dogen, the thirteenth-century founder of Soto Zen, writes: "This realm of reality is also called enlightenment, and it is also called the inconceivable realm. It is also called wisdom and it is also called not being born and not passing away. Thus all phenomena are not other than the realm of reality; hearing of this nonduality and nondifference, do not give rise to doubt." A place where there is nothing on which to dwell. A silent realm of reality, known (and unknown) in moments of enlightenment.

There is no distinction to be made between the experience of this world and transcendent meaning. Appearance, in the fullness (or emptiness) of awareness in the here and now, is all the meaning in the world. With enlightenment, there is nothing that has to be done.

Only with the dropping off of the self is the nature of all things revealed. As Francis Cook, in his book *Sounds of Valley Streams,* writes in a commentary on Dogen, "Reality is nothing but that which we encounter in the absence of the craving, fear, sentimentality, prejudice, discrimination, and judgment that originates in the small self." In other words, reality is experienced when the self (the ego-self) is lost. Then we are enlightened and opened to the reality. An enlightenment that is more than mere satisfaction about the nature of reality; an enlightenment that liberates this human being. A freedom to be at one with the world.

Lives, then, are lived spontaneously without the weight of consequences for oneself. "For this reason, compassion is a very simple matter; one forgets the self and does what is needed," Cook writes. We have thus moved from the search for reality—the craving for reality—to the living of a compassionate life. A compassionate life lived simply by acting in accord with awareness of our oneness with all others and with all things—beyond self, beyond the knowing self. The end is compassion, and the elimination of suffering, rather than knowing reality. Without effort, reality is fully experienced.

Alan Watts writes in his book *The Way of Liberation,* "If you want life, do not cling to it, let it go." And in the phraseology of Zen Buddhism, "You cannot achieve this by thinking, you cannot achieve this by not thinking." We watch the trains go by. We watch, we photograph, we listen—this is our practice for the time being.

The last roll of film from my winter of wandering is being developed. Black and white, night and day, the noise and the silence, the freezing and the melting, loneliness and companionship, life and death—each comes with the other. The lesson of ecology, the lesson of no separate self, is that all things are interdependent and that finally all things are one. May I neither dwell nor not dwell on the question of reality again. This I have learned during the passing of another year.

III.

The years are passing and the trains are still speeding through town with blasting horns. Physically the town looks about the same, although a few more of the stores on Lincoln Highway have closed and the buildings stand vacant. I am not bothered nearly as much by the sounds of the trains. Photographing with a certain frame of mind and keeping notes have been a cure of sorts.

This project came to me, out of need, as I intentionally let myself be open to the questions of existence. My position was one of being on the edge, of being vulnerable to the world. Rather than pretending to be an observer who had it all under control, I opened myself to both the wonder and the horror of existing in a vast and ultimately unknowable universe. I was an observer of a place, a reader of the texts of others, a photographer of abstracted black and white images, a sometime participant in one community or another, a philosopher of everyday life, and a householder. Many voices at once, but such is the price and the reward of letting things happen as they may.

Likely I will soon be leaving this town. I have hopes of a new beginning. The purpose ultimately is to know how to live compassionately. Knowledge as a practical social skill rather than as an intellectual enterprise. The emphasis, still existential, is on action and a life of participation in the world.

The persistent human problem is that of finding a home in this world. In his book *At Home in the World,* Michael Jackson, while engaged in ethnographic fieldwork, turns our existential attention to the problem of home. Home is a lived relationship, he argues, rather than an entity or essence. "Knowledge then becomes a way of carrying us into more fruitful and caring relationships with others, rather than distancing ourselves from others in the name of objectivity." Knowledge is thus a form of worldly immanence, being with others, here and now. Instead of being alienated from the world, we are at home in the world with others. The whistle no longer seems to be the loneliest or loudest of calls. We are at home in the world together.

The century is ending. Our time is marked arbitrarily by the calendar. Days into months, months into years, and years into centuries. "Where were we before we were born?" a Zen master asks. And where will we be when we are no longer here? A brief moment of mortal existence, and more a wonder for all of that. Struck by awe and incapable of knowing the meaning of our existence, we go on. Our faith is in the wonder of our daily lives. In a human community of compassion with others. We continue, as pilgrims, keeping records, making notes, and photographing what we see in this sublime world of our common existence.

Bibliography

Agee, James, and Walker Evans. *Let Us Now Praise Famous Men.* Boston: Houghton Mifflin, 1941.

Auden, W. H. *Collected Poems.* Ed. Edward Mendelson. New York: Vintage Books, 1991.

Bachelard, Gaston. *The Poetics of Space.* Trans. Maria Jolas. Boston: Beacon Press, 1969.

Barthes, Roland. *Camera Lucida: Reflections on Photography.* Trans. Richard Howard. New York: Hill and Wang, 1981.

Bashō, Matsuo. *The Narrow Road to the Deep North and Other Travel Essays.* Trans. Nobuyuki Yuasa. New York: Penguin, 1966.

Batchelor, Stephen. *Alone with Others: An Existential Approach to Buddhism.* New York: Grove Press, 1983.

Beckett, Samuel. *I Can't Go On, I'll Go On.* Ed. Richard Seaver. New York: Grove Press, 1976.

Benjamin, Walter. *The Arcades Project.* Trans. Howard Eiland and Kevin McLaughlin. Cambridge, MA: Harvard University Press, 1999.

Berger, John, and Jean Mohr. *A Fortunate Man.* New York: Pantheon Books, 1967.

Bernanos, Georges. *The Diary of a Country Priest.* Trans. Pamela Morris. New York: Carroll and Greb Publishers, 1983. First published in 1937.

Berry, Wendell. *Sabbaths.* San Francisco: North Point Press, 1987.

Blanchot, Maurice. *The Space of Literature.* Trans. Ann Smock. Lincoln: University of Nebraska Press, 1982.

Bowles, Paul. *Days: Tangier Journal, 1987–1989.* New York: Ecco Press, 1991.

Burke, Edmund. *A Philosophical Enquiry into the Origin of Our Ideas of the Sublime and Beautiful.* Ed. J. T. Boulton. London: Routledge and Kegan Paul, 1958. First published in 1857.

Burton, Robert. *The Anatomy of Melancholy.* 8th ed. Philadelphia: J. W. Moore, 1857.

Byron, Thomas. *The Heart of Awareness: A Translation of the Ashtavakra Gita.* Boston: Shambhala, 1990.

Camus, Albert. *American Journals.* Trans. Hugh Levick. New York: Paragon House, 1987.

Camus, Albert. *The Fall.* Trans. Justin O'Brien. New York: Vintage Books, 1991.

Camus, Albert. *The Myth of Sisyphus and Other Essays.* Trans. Justin O'Brien. New York: Alfred A. Knopf, 1991.

Camus, Albert. *Notebooks, 1942–1951.* Trans. Justin O'Brien. New York: Paragon House, 1991.

Camus, Albert. *The Stranger.* Trans. Matthew Ward. New York: Alfred A. Knopf, 1993.

Cavell, Stanley. *The Senses of Walden.* San Francisco: North Point Press, 1981.

Chah, Achaan. *A Still Forest Pool.* Ed. Jack Kornfield and Paul Breiter. Wheaton, IL: Theosophical Publishing House, 1985.

Chaucer, Geoffrey. *The Canterbury Tales.* Trans. Nevill Coghill. Baltimore: Penguin Books, 1962.

Cleary, Thomas, ed. and trans. *Zen Essences: The Science of Freedom.* Boston: Shambhala, 1989.

Coleridge, Samuel Taylor. *The Rime of the Ancient Mariner.* Ed. Paul H. Fry. Boston: Bedford/St.Martin's, 1999.

Cook, Francis H. *Sounds of Valley Streams: Enlightenment in Dogen's Zen.* Albany: State University of New York Press, 1989.

Dhammapada, The. Trans. Eknath Easwaran. Petaluma, CA: Nilgiri Press, 1985.

Dürckheim, Karlfried. *The Way of Transformation: Daily Life as Spiritual Exercise.* London: George Allen and Unwin, 1971.

Eckhart, Meister. *Meister Eckhart: A Modern Translation.* Trans. Raymond Bernard Blakney. New York: Harper, 1957.

Eliot, T. S. *The Complete Poems and Plays.* London: Faber and Faber, 1969.

Emerson, Ralph Waldo. *Ralph Waldo Emerson: Essays and Lectures.* Ed. Joel Porte. New York: Library of America, 1983.

Flanagan, John T. "Thoreau in Minnesota." *Minnesota History* 16 (March 1935): 35-46.

Goethe, Johann Wolfgang von. *Italian Journey, 1786–1788.* Trans. W. H. Auden and Elizabeth Mayer. San Francisco: North Point Press, 1982.

Goldstein, Joseph, and Jack Kornfield. *Seeking the Heart of Wisdom.* Boston: Shambhala, 1987.

Hammarskjöld, Dag. *Markings.* Trans. Leif Sjoberg and W. H. Auden. New York: Alfred A. Knopf, 1964.

Hanh, Thich Nhat. *Being Peace.* Berkeley: Parallax Press, 1987.

Hanh, Thich Nhat. *No Death, No Fear.* New York: Riverhead Books, 2002.

Hanh, Thich Nhat. *Peace Is Every Step.* New York: Bantam Books, 1991.

Jackson, Michael. *At Home in the World.* Durham, NC: Duke University Press, 1995.

Joyce, James. *Dubliners.* New York: Viking Penguin, 1976.

Joyce, James. *Ulysses.* New York: Modern Library, 1992.

Kant, Immanuel. *Critique of Judgement.* New York: Hafner Press, 1951.

Kierkegaard, Søren. *The Diary of Søren Kierkegaard.* Ed. Peter P. Rohde. New York: Philosophical Library, 1960.

Koerner, Joseph Leo. *Caspar David Friedrich and the Subject of Landscape.* New Haven, CT: Yale University Press, 1990.

Krishnamurti, J. *Freedom from the Known.* New York: Harper & Row, 1975.

Krishnamurti, J. *Krishnamurti's Notebook.* New York: Harper & Row, 1976.

Lagerkvist, Pär. *Evening Land.* Trans. Anthony Barnett. East Sussex, UK: Allardyce Book, 2001.

Lao-tzu. *Tao Te Ching*. Trans. Stephen Mitchell. New York: Harper & Row, 1988.

Lehrman, Fredric. *The Sacred Landscape*. Berkeley, CA: Celestial Arts, 1988.

Li Po. *The Selected Poems of Li Po*. Trans. David Hinton. New York: New Directions, 1996.

Maezremi, Hakruyu Taizan. *The Way of Everyday Life*. Los Angeles: Zen Center, 1978.

Merton, Thomas. *Thoughts on Solitude*. New York: Farrar, Straus and Giroux, 1958.

Merton, Thomas. *The Way of Chuang Tzu*. New York: New Directions, 1965.

Nietzsche, Friedrich. *The Gay Science*. Trans. Walter Kaufmann. New York: Vintage Books, 1974.

Nietzsche, Friedrich. *Thus Spoke Zarathustra*. Trans. Walter Kaufmann. New York: Viking Books, 1978.

Nishitani, Keiji. *Religion and Nothingness*. Trans. Jan Van Bragt. Berkeley: University of California Press, 1982.

Noyes, Russell, ed. *English Romantic Poetry and Prose*. New York: Oxford University Press, 1956.

Pushkin, Alexander. Boris Godunov. Trans. Alfred Hayes. New York: Dutton, 1918.

Quinney, Richard. *Borderland: A Midwest Journal*. Madison: University of Wisconsin Press, 2001.

Quinney, Richard. *For the Time Being: Ethnography of Everyday Life*. Albany: State University Press of New York, 1998.

Quinney, Richard. *Journey to a Far Place: Autobiographical Reflections*. Philadelphia: Temple University Press, 1991.

Reps, Paul. *Zen Flesh, Zen Bones*. New York: Penguin, 1971.

Rewald, Sabine, ed. *The Romantic Vision of Caspar David Friedrich*. New York: Metropolitan Museum of Art, 1990.

Richardson, Robert D. *Henry Thoreau: A Life of the Mind*. Berkeley: University of California Press, 1986.

Rilke, Rainer Maria. *Letters to a Young Poet*. Trans. Stephen Mitchell. Boston: Shambhala, 1993.

Rilke, Rainer Maria. *The Selected Poetry of Rainer Maria Rilke*. Ed. and trans. Stephen Mitchell. New York: Random House, 1982.

Ryōkan. *One Robe, One Bowl: The Zen Poetry of Ryōkan*. Trans. John Stevens. New York: Weatherhill, 1977.

Seung Sahn. *Only Don't Know*. San Francisco: Four Seasons, 1982.

Shakespeare, William. *The Sonnets and Narrative Poems*. New York: Alfred A. Knopf, 1992.

Shelley, Percy Bysshe. "Mont Blanc." In *Shelley: Selected Poetry and Prose*. New York: Routledge, 1991.

Sontag, Susan. *On Photography*. New York: Farrar, Straus and Giroux, 1973.

Sudek, Josef. *Josef Sudek, Poet of Prague: A Photographer's Life*. Biographical profile by Anna Farova. New York: Aperture, 1990.

Suzuki, Shunryu. *Zen Mind, Beginner's Mind*. New York: Weatherhill, 1970.

Szarkowski, John. *Looking at Photographs*. New York: Museum of Modern Art, 1973.

Tennyson, Alfred Lord. "In Memoriam." In M. H. Abrams, ed., *The Norton Anthology of English Literature*, 5th ed., New York: W. W. Norton, 1987.

Thoreau, Henry D. *The Correspondence of Henry David Thoreau*. Ed. Walter Harding and Carl Bode. New York: New York University Press, 1958.

Thoreau, Henry D. *The Journal of Henry D. Thoreau*. Ed. Bradford Torrey and Francis H. Allen. Vol. 14. Boston: Houghton Mifflin, 1949.

Thoreau, Henry D. *Walden*. Ed. J. Lyndon Shanley. Princeton: Princeton University Press, 1973.

Tuan, Yi-Fu. *Space and Place*. Minneapolis: University of Minnesota Press, 1977.

Twitchell, James B. *Romantic Horizons: Aspects of the Sublime in English Poetry and Painting, 1770-1850*. Columbia: University of Missouri Press, 1983.

Upanishads, The. Trans. Juan Mascaró. New York: Penguin, 1965.

Vendler, Helen. *The Art of Shakespeare's Sonnets.* Cambridge, MA: Harvard University Press, 1997.

Wang, Wei. *Laughing Lost in the Mountains: Poems of Wang Wei.* Trans. Tony Barnstone, Willis Barnstone, and Xu Haixin. Hanover, NH: University Press of New England, 1991.

Warner, Rex. *The Stories of the Greeks.* New York: Farrar, Straus and Giroux, 1967.

Watts, Alan. *The Way of Liberation: Essays and Lectures on the Transformation of Self.* Ed. Mark Watts and Rebecca Shropshire. New York: Weatherhill, 1983.

Watts, Isaac. *The Psalms and Hymns of Isaac Watts.* Morgan, PA: Soli Deo Gloria, 1997.

White, Minor. *Minor White: Rites and Passages.* Biographical essay by James Becker Hall. New York: Aperture, 1978.

Wilton, Andrew. *Turner and the Sublime.* London: British Museum Publications, 1980.

Wittgenstein, Ludwig. *Tractatus Logico-Philosophicus.* Trans. C. K. Ogden. London: Routledge and Kegan Paul, 1981.

Wordsworth, William. *The Poems of William Wordsworth.* Ed. Jonathan Wordsworth. Cambridge, UK: University Printing House, 1973.

Wright, Charles. *The World of Ten Thousand Things, Poems 1980–1990.* New York: Farrar Straus Giroux, 1990.

Yeats, W. B., ed. *Fairy and Folk Tales of Ireland.* New York: Modern Library, 1994.

About the Author

Richard Quinney is the author of several books of autobiographical writing, including *Journey to a Far Place, For the Time Being, Borderland, Once Again the Wonder, Where Yet the Sweet Birds Sing, Tales from the Middle Border, Field Notes, A Lifetime Burning, Once Upon an Island, A Farm in Wisconsin,* and *Ox Herding in Wisconsin.* His retrospective book of photographs, *Things Once Seen,* received the August Derleth Award from the Council of Wisconsin Writers. His other books are in the field of sociology. He lives in Madison, Wisconsin.

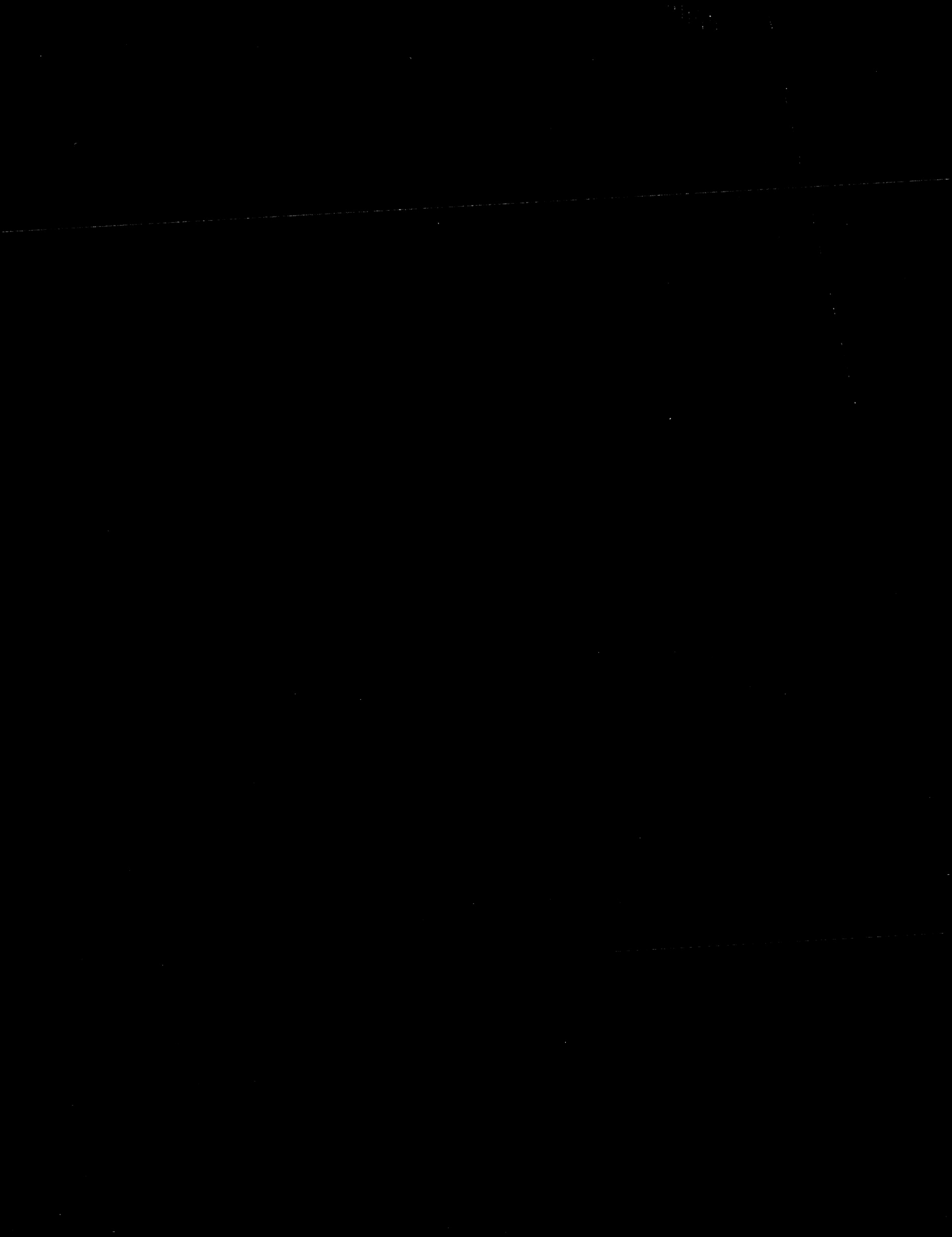